HOME FURNISHINGS
MERCHANDISING
& STORE DESIGN

HOME FURNISHINGS
MERCHANDISING
& STORE DESIGN

Edited by Martin M. Pegler

Retail Reporting Corporation, New York

Retail Reporting Corporation
101 Fifth Avenue
New York, NY 10003

Distributors to the trade in the United States and Canada:
Van Nostrand Reinhold
115 Fifth Avenue
New York, NY 10003

Distributed outside of the United States and Canada:
Hearst Books International
105 Madison Avenue
New York, NY 10016

Library of Congress Cataloging in Publication Data:
Main Entry under the title: Home Furnishings Merchandising & Store Design

Printed and Bound in Hong Kong
ISBN 0-934590-36-2

Designed by Judy Shepard

Contents

The retail field of Home Furnishings has come a long, long way, and as we enter the last ten years of the twentieth century, we are hearing buzz words and phrases like "cocooning" and "the decade of the home." When "you've gone about as far as you can go" — it is always nice to know that there is still "no place like home." For years we've gone through "generations" that ranged from "hippie" — to "me" — to "us"; and now it seems, at last, it is time for the "Home Generation." In the past the way to show how successful you were was to have the foreign sportscars lined up in the driveway tagged with vanity plates and maybe even a cabin cruiser on wheels and discretely semi-draped with a tarpaulin. Today, we are moving our affluence indoors.

With more and more family units consisting of two working adults, with people rushing about all day, the quiet, comfort and security of a few hours at home become special. To counteract the rushing and pushing of the daytime hours, friends and families come together around the "hearth" which is more often than not a giant entertainment center. Why go out to see a movie when you can bring the movie in. Theater, opera and sporting events are as close as the clicker on the VCR pad, and you can see it clearer and larger on the big screen that is now part of the home environment.

The "empty nest syndrome" we read about, — of parents in their 50s and 60s suddenly on their own and finding themselves with more discretionary income has led to "the second time around" home — or the "second" home. Older persons are redoing their homes or moving into newer, smaller quarters and these new accommodations are usually lighter, brighter, and more care-free in concept. They are getting rid of their "clutter" and opening up their homes just as they are opening up their lives. Those young persons who have left "the nest" are now starting "nests" of their own and they need furniture and furnishings that will grow with them, — with their needs, — and with their growing families.

More and more, people are moving their businesses into their homes. The newspapers and home fashion magazines are showing examples and offering editorial recommendations as to how to turn a den into a tax-exemption office, — and all it seems to take is a phone, a file and a fax.

With so much emphasis on the home and the furnishing of the home, we present this volume of outstanding designs of spaces and stores involved in the presentation of furniture and furnishings for the home. Our emphasis is twofold. Not only is the store design and layout important, the visual merchandising and display techniques involved are equally vital to the success of the retail space. Our examples balance space with product presentation, and always show how the physical environment is adapted to the creation of an ambience or fashion attitude that enhances the merchandise on the floor — on the walls — or on the platforms.

This volume, for the sake of reference and identification has been divided into five chapters. Retail classifications have become so vague and so general that it is almost impossible to distinguish between a department store, a specialty store or a chain of related, but not necessarily contiguous shops that together could be called a department store because of the range and depth of product categories presented. A free standing Ralph Lauren Polo store, like the one on Madison Ave. in NYC is more than a designer's boutique. It could be called a department/specialty store because in addition to clothing for the entire family, the store also carries Lauren designed sheets and pillow cases, bed and bathroom ensembles and even home furnishings and decorative accessories. Rather than call it a department store, we would call it a life-style store since everything there is targeted at a particular customer and the merchandise personifies a particular life-style, — a way of living and looking. At a different level, Marks & Spenser, the popular English chain long noted for good sweaters and sensible underwear, has now reached out into the Home Furnishings field and they have turned what was a fashion specialty store into a life-style oriented department store often equipped with a food market. Thus, — our selections are grouped into definitely debatable chapters. What we call one store might, to the reader's way of thinking, be not as appropriate as some other title, but let's not quibble; it really isn't that important. What is relevant and we hope apparent in our selections and what we say about them is what is happening in the field of Home Furnishing.

As you read the text you will in many instances find quotes. Sometimes we quote the architects/designers and show the problems or goals of the project, and they may explain the "what, why and how" of the solutions arrived at. Wherever possible we have also tried to include words of the retailers; we have allowed them to explain what makes them, their merchandise and their concepts of presentation unique in this very competitive field, and what they hoped the store design would do for them.

The target market, the retailer's and the merchandise's image, and the fashion attitude are indicated in the text, where possible because if one picture is worth a thousand words, a hundred or so of appropriate words can frame and enhance the picture so that it speaks volumes.

Martin M. Pegler, S.V.M. / ASID / ISP

Chapter One

Showrooms are exhibit areas where presentation is paramount. This is not where a single bedroom ensemble is purchased after an hour or two of self-debate or where a roomful of carpeting is selected. The showroom is big business; it is where volume orders are recorded, — where retailers or designers must be convinced that the products on display will not only sell in quantity or serve their functions, — but they will excel in both areas.

In this chapter we are showing both retail and contract showrooms, but the task for either showroom is to convince an expert, a knowledgeable "customer," that what is being offered is the best that is available and will be successful. Our showrooms include those open to merchandisers, to the chain or specialty store buyers where the coordinated products are presented with theatrical expertise in idealized settings under professional stage lighting and in an atmosphere that will enhance the product and also compliment the taste level of the merchandisers for having selected to purchase these products. This is "stroke and sell." Other showrooms, in this chapter, have been designed to convince architects and designers in the contract furnishing field. These are specialists who will not be taken in by lighting techniques and stage-y settings. They come seeking information and solutions. They want to sample the full range of product, — the infinite variety, — the colors and textures. They want to see and touch and try, — be intimately involved with the product and see more than just an assembled spectacle. Here the architectural ambience is set back so that the product steps forward and the lights must be telling and revealing light rather than an illusion of stage craft.

Combined with Showrooms, in this chapter, are Galleries. A gallery usually suggests a museum or an exhibit area and, in a way, these retail operations have tried to bring Art into Furnishings. The chapter includes several operations, on both coasts, that are in the business of selling Functional Art: furniture and furnishings, — one-of-a-kind or of limited editions, created by artists, architects, designers and craftspersons. These pieces are unique and expensive, and the retail settings are designed to enhance that look and also suggest that these are collector items and not just something to squat on or use to light up a corner. The retail spaces are open and airy, the products are raised up on platforms and the galleries are carefully lit to create an ambience and also highlight the pieces. Two actual galleries have been included in this collection since "Art" is today part of home furnishings. The Mexican gallery sells paintings and sculpture in a subdued, romantic atmosphere while the Melrose Ave. one mixes wall and cabinet art with functional art in a bright space filled with funky flair. In the Specialty Store chapter there are other gallery-type retail set-ups.

Other retail operations in this chapter are designed to suggest showrooms rather than retail stores. When the viewer examines a manufacturer's showroom like Cannon Mills and compares it to the mall prototype store developed by Sheridan, he/she will immediately see how effective that sort of "showroom" setting can be when combined with the well packaged stock for an upscale product. Most of the products presented in the retail establishments in this chapter are upscaled: As the reader will perceive, the store designs are subtle understatements, the colors are generally neutral and the textures and materials though often quite ordinary speak elegance in the simplicity with which they are used. Lighting plays an even more important role in these operations than it would in the traditional home furnishings store.

F. Schumacher & Co.
Third Ave., NYC

F. Schumacher & Co.

Design: The Phillips Janson Group, NY

vated; today this showroom is open to the "trade," — for the pleasure and perusal of designers and architects.

The fabric, wallcoverings and floor coverings are contained in "rooms" off a long, classic arcade enriched with Tuscan columns flanking the openings to the display areas, arches and vaulted ceilings. The client enters into a peach and cream marble rotunda, warm and elegant, and capped by a series of rising rings of light. Brass letters set into the arched entablatures indicate which product world lies ahead. "Our ideas was to create a showroom space that is a very specific showcase for our product — a space that makes things easier to find and that is a comfortable place for our designers to work in," said Philip P. Puschel, Schumacher's president and C.E.O.

According to the designers of the showroom, "the traditional residential architecture enhances the established image of the fabric, floor and wallcoverings,

This famous American firm has been manufacturing and importing quality textiles for the past 100 years and the history of Schumacher's is representative of the history of the decorative textile business in this country for the same period of time.

It is a far step in time but only a few miles from Frederick Schumacher's first shop on 22nd St. and Broadway to the almost street-long Museum of Fabrics that has been recreated in their 15,000 square foot showroom, in Bloomingdale country on Third Ave and E. 56th St. Back then it was the "carriage trade" that was culti-

while the gallery-like layouts showcase each Schumacher product line. The importance and imagery of the products are further emphasized by the natural museum quality lighting.''

Project Principal-in-charge:
  James G. Phillips, AIA
Design Principal-in-charge:
  Frederic M. Strauss, AIA
Project Designer: Fred F. Rodriguez
Dir. of Construction: Susan A. Dennison
Photos: Jaime Ardiles-Arce

Maharam

would make a dramatic statement and also display the product to its best advantage.

The result, shown here, is the simple drama of a glass parallelogram surrounding an all-black interior. Inside, the stark space is defined only by a series of free-standing geometric cubes and cylinders that indicate the circulation route and also are the sole furnishings/display elements on the floor. The ingenious split forms offer exhibit capacity on both sides and allows more than 15,000 units of fabrics to be presented. A centrally located split cylinder displays upholstery and wall covering swatches, with drapery fabrics hung from two split cubes.

When Maharam, the largest fabric house in the United States, acquired a six-sided, narrow, glass-walled space of 1500 square feet in the Pacific Design Center, the firm was concerned that its space would be overpowered by the imposing designs of the surrounding showrooms. The company turned to the designer and it became his task to create an environment that

The effect of colorful fabrics against black is enhanced by low voltage, high intensity beam light fixtures which draw attention to the product display. The hard architectural surfaces and dark background offer maximum contrast to the look and feel of the fabrics.

Designer: George Kaneko

13

Collins & Aikman

Design: Eva Maddox Associates, Inc., Chicago, IL

For the past seven years the Collins & Aikman company retained Eva Maddox Associates as interior design consultants to the Floor Covering division. The design company's services have included the architectural concept, interior design, product design and carpet technology research, color analysis design and product styling for creating total interior environment to promote the company.

The Collins & Aikman conference center and showroom was designed within a formal ordering system, utilizing simple volumes to create a sense of space. The perimeter circulation allowed for access and also maximized the use of space. The design itself draws inspiration from the "Viennese Secession principle of integrating design on every level and incorporates exquisite detailing to complete the space."

There is an elegant use of softly bowed

arcs with fine vertical elements to counteract the sweep. The walls are warm, off-white and black is used to accent, to outline and to delineate surfaces and planes. The furniture is finished in black lacquer. Since the showroom was established to show contract floor coverings, the designers created unique flooring designs with standard materials and these floor covering concepts were used to establish orientation and traffic patterns for the visitors as well as extend the overall design statement. Thus, the visitor can not only study the material at eye level, but also appreciate it as part of the underfoot pattern.

Photos: Nick Merrick / Hedrick-Blessing

Thybony

Merchandise Mart, Chicago, IL

Design: Eva Maddox Associates, Inc., Chicago, IL

This fabric and wallcovering showroom is located at the end of a dimly lit corridor, and the designers introduced lightly colored materials and accent lighting to make the showroom visible, — and to attract viewer attention.

The guest is invited in through a classical iron gate. Angled partitions with offset window displays create a rhythmic sequence on either side of the entry. The plan for the showroom is simple with the architecture serving as a background for the products. The showroom needed to be

functional and have designer work areas as well as house ample sampling. Circulation space with alcoves allows point-to-point interest throughout the showroom and small, intimate rooms are provided for viewing individual product types. The showroom contains many different kinds of fabric displays: fabric as art, banners, window screens, actual wallcoverings in space, upholstered products, fabric covered wall panels, as well as the traditional flip wings. In the rear of the showroom, a customer service desk also doubles as a product display. The bright

display of multi-colored fabric samples built into the millworked desk acts as a draw to bring the viewer to this rear area.

To keep the showroom timeless and fresh, a contemporary environment was achieved through the use of materials. Hand made Mexican tile floors provide a feeling of warmth and texture, and they contrast against the white walls. Gray highlights and periwinkle blue accents complete the color scheme.

Photos: Timothy Long, Chicago, IL

MDC Wallcoverings

Design: Eva Maddox Associates, Inc., Chicago, IL

The underlying grid structure that was designed by EMA is first expressed at the entry and through the repetition of the colonnade. As the visitor passes through the colonnade and becomes impressed by the intimacy affected by its lowered ceiling plane, he/she is directed towards a dynamic red overhead beam that supports all elements of separation. "The design statement expresses an ordered spacial experience and a rational design approach."

Throughout the space, unexpected relationships focus attention onto a variety of products. Horizontal and vertical planes coverage to one point perspective at all planes. The radial tubular display unit on the wall is repeated in the grid in 6" to 12" increments and the string grid serves to unify disparate elements. Black becomes the foil for the soft tactile qualities and the strong colors of the products. The walls of swatches make a tremendous color impact on the viewer and they also reinforce the fact that there is a wide range of fabrics and colors to choose from.

The floors are large squares of light and dark gray, and the walls and ceilings are black. Columns and partitions are painted shiny black or deep gray and the overhead grid holds the spotlights. In the long display corridor where the product walls are gridded in black, the lights in the ceilings, over the gray gridded floors, bring the sample colors to brilliant life.

Photos: Orlando Cabanban, Chicago, IL

Lee's Commercial Carpet Co.

Merchandise Mart, Chicago, IL

Design: Fitch-RichardsonSmith, Worthington, OH

The entire 6,000 square feet of space was designed around the theme of ''Creating Floors.'' The principal objective was to create an environment that built on Lee's credibility and reputation, and that dramatically introduced heightened and enhanced design sensitivity. The designers had to establish a sense of theater as a point of differentiation; to encourage participation from a broad audience base, and make a lasting impression. With no wall-to-wall carpeting and no product displayed on the floor, the showroom is a unique display of minimalism.

Two exterior glass walls, facing the main corridors, are painted opaquely to match the interior color palette. At spaced intervals, clear glass ''windows'' invite spectators to look inside. In addition to the up front twenty-four foot signature wall with the three dimensional Lee's logo, there are strong sightlines in all directions. A stark curved wall becomes a dramatic backdrop for a 25'x40' ''sidewalk'' where artists perform and customers are invited to join in the creative process. The showroom contains a series of carefully balanced feature areas: the artistry in action (on the

sidewalk), ten activity hubs which encourage participation with new products, and enhance interaction with the sales staff, new and existing product displays and a quiet consultation space and reception area.

The activity hubs range in size from five feet square to 10'x30', and the glass topped tables in the areas incorporate chalk boards so that customers can create while they discuss their needs. The especially designed area rugs in each hub add impetus to the underlying theme of creating floors.

A simple product display using a galvanized metal framework presents all carpet tile products in a square format and broadloom samples are shown in rectangular forms. The full line of colors and products is displayed in one location.

Design Team Project Director: Lee Svet
Designer: P. Kelly Mooney
Photos: Steve Trank
Client Design Team: Robt. D. Hutchinson,
V.P., Product Development
Art Source: Ann Joyce & Jan O'Dea

J.&J. Industries

Merchandise Mart, Chicago, IL

Design: Fitch-RichardsonSmith, Worthington, OH

What J.&J. had in mind for their showroom in the Merchandise Mart was an environment that would reproduce the feelings and qualities of a tour in an actual carpet mill. The showroom had to display their product in a manner that would specifically appeal to the many people who come to the all-important Neocon show, — and it all had to be implemented within strict budget parameters.

Fitch-RichardsonSmith was able to gather a collection of interesting artifacts from the actual mill and incorporate them into the design of the showroom. The reproduction of a loom allowed customers to walk under "dancing" fibers, and they could experience the actual feel and touch of the materials. Photographs of the artifacts "in action" also enhanced the gallery feeling.

The loom was constructed of white pine beams bolted together with the carpet fibers fed around white horizontal tubes made of PVC tubing. The large carpet fiber spools were actual beams from the mill.

The carpet samples were glued and wrapped around cardboard tubes of different diameters and lengths. The geometrics' end caps were made of painted particle board and the display platform for the carpet display tubes was fabricated out of MDO plywood.

The columns on the floor were incorporated into the "mill" design with yarns and fibers collected in semi-circular bins. On some of the perimeter walls, sample swatches were attached to panels to facilitate the distribution of samples.

The white walls and a medium gray carpet were capped with a black ceiling which was filled with long stretches of black track lighting. The incandescent spots added warmth and sparkle to the colored products displayed on the walls, and on the open free-to-walk floors.

Elements By Grapevine

Design: Ganner Inc., Dallas, TX

Elements By Grapevine is a rapidly growing manufacturer of furniture from the San Joaquin area of California whose success has been tied in with the company's innovative designs, its resourcefulness in the use of unusual materials and its bright, one-step-ahead design capabilities. Their collections go way beyond the usual furniture materials to include California grapevines for table bases as well as imaginative couplings of faux stone finishes, exotic woods and marble. "We are not doing conventional wood furniture so we're a little controversial," says Renee Kubryk, co-founder and design director of the company. "We're more artistic and decorative than functional. In our price range there's very little that's unusual."

To showcase their unique designs, the owners invited Ray Ganner of Ganner, Inc. to design their High Point showroom. To complement the natural materials and the often muted colors of the designs, the designer opted for a setting of taupe/gray flooring and off-white walls, and arranged the tables and accessories as art pieces in gallery-like settings. The area is alive with natural flowers and plants, — all part of the natural quality of the furniture designs and materials.

The motivating philosophy behind Elements By Grapevine is to offer something new and unusual every market, — "to give people something to talk about. We do lots of textural, earthy things that you want to reach out and touch and we've taken finishes a few steps up." The free moving circulation of the showroom allows shoppers to wander from grouping to grouping. Some are housed in semistructures while others are separated into on-the-floor clusters that are identified by the spotlights that are located all over the blacked out ceiling. Up-lights, on the columns, are the only other source of illumination in the showroom. The customers are invited to see, touch and smell the taste that is Elements By Grapevine.

Steelcase / Stowe & Davis

Merchandise Mart, Chicago, IL

Design: Robert Blaha, Steelcase Inc. / Lohan & Assoc., Chicago, IL

Steelcase commissioned Lohan & Associates to transfer the 28,000 square foot space into a classic environment which would be used to introduce "Context," a new free-standing furniture system. The primary design goal was to showcase Steelcase's products in an interior sensitive to Chicago's architectural heritage. Particular to this show was the idea of a fictitious "Company" and the floor plan was configured to replicate the office setting of an entire staff of that make-believe company, — showing the many applications of the system to satisfy the many different office activities and the persons who work in those offices.

The showroom covers two floors in the Mart and the remarkable tubular steel staircase that connects the floors becomes a focal element in the design. It is a functional piece of sculpture set against the

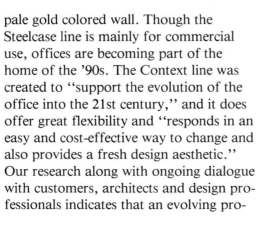

pale gold colored wall. Though the Steelcase line is mainly for commercial use, offices are becoming part of the home of the '90s. The Context line was created to "support the evolution of the office into the 21st century," and it does offer great flexibility and "responds in an easy and cost-effective way to change and also provides a fresh design aesthetic." Our research along with ongoing dialogue with customers, architects and design professionals indicates that an evolving pro-

fessional workforce has created a need for a variety of work settings to accomplish different tasks. The group of offices on the floor not only suggest what specialized activities can be accommodated by Context, but the layout also says something about the person who "occupies" each space.

Other vignette displays and work areas are included in the layout of the showroom and light, decorative transluscent panels serve to divide the work spaces.

Gunlocke

Design: Walker Group / CNI, NY

The designers were called upon to design a fully integrated 12,000 square foot contract furniture showroom which would respond to the client's increasing product line and growth in the marketplace. It was to be a "sophisticated yet not imposing architectural 'foil' which would work in tandem with as well as enhance the products on display."

The plan involved the utilization of the ex-isting structural grid of columns augmented with a secondary 45 degree dissecting grid. This dual concept was applied to both the floor and ceiling layouts. An informal appearance was achieved with wide terrazzo aisles and carpeted merchandise islands. The space was further divided into two equal halves, emphasized by means of the aisle pattern and expressed lighting track, — providing a subliminal directional message to the

visitors. The rear panelled walls separate the main showroom from the ancillary areas. Two conference rooms with rear projection facilities, a Training/Presentation area and a comprehensive samples wall accommodate the necessary hands on approach to furniture selection.

The color scheme of pale ceilings; taupe, black and white textured walls; mauve automotive metallic painted rear wall paneling; black, gray and yellow terrazzo and gray/yellow carpeting provide a strong architectural background which seems neutral when juxtaposed with the rich finish of the product.

Partner-in-charge: Joanne Newbold
Project Executive/Designer: David Wales
For Gunlocke: Don Keith, V.P., Marketing

Mikasa

Design: Joseph Fleece, V.P. Product Development

In an historic Cast Iron building in the revitalized Flatiron district is located the vast, "to the trade" showroom for Mikasa and its many divisions and sub-divisions. The space is long, wide and high with 18' columns to form a grid pattern on the floor. The customer enters into a long, dramatically lit gallery of Mikasa dinnerware settings set out with the appropriate Mikasa stemware and silverware on sleek, black lacquered shelves. The saw-tooth arrangement of the tall, off-white walls tends to divide each group into a special and individual presentation. On the opposite side, black mirrored panels serve to back up the table settings in which the products are artfully arranged by color and pattern on tabletops, and large graphic panels explain what is being coordinated. The floor is also sleek black, tiled, and the only light is from the spotlights directed at the groupings on the wall and the tabletop settings.

Partway back is a curved wall with black niches that house samples of Mikasa glass

and crystal giftware. On the floor, in glass pyramid shaped etageres are more of the crystal pieces treated as unique and "museum" quality. Raised up several steps — on a mezzanine — is the designer collection by Oscar de la Renta and some pieces by Erte. The former's designs are arranged on festively designed table tops with the china, stemware and flatware all coordinated. The Erte collection contains service plates and dinnerware.

In addition, towards the rear of the show-room space which is almost a full city block deep, there are more casual and relaxed presentations of the Studio Nova and Savoir-Vivre divisions which include houseware lines, china, holloware and plastics. The Home Beautiful line, for mass merchants, is also on display here in color coordinated groupings on the walls and on the floor in colorful vignettes which use appropriate pieces of furniture to create the desired ambience for the products.

Photos: Martin M. Pegler

J.P. Stevens

Louis Nichole Showroom at J.P. Stevens, Mikel Wenslow, Visual Merchandising Director

To introduce a new line of bed and bath designs by the noted home furnishings designer, Louis Nichole, the entrance was converted into a mini-Versailles. The narrow aisle was enriched with Ionic piers flanking the entrances to the exhibit areas, and white rubbed boiserie panels filled in the walls between. Over the rich terracotta colored carpet was laid an Aubusson type runner to introduce the pastels and floral patterns to be presented beyond. At the end of the aisle, a mirrored wall and an exuberant arrangement of silk flowers in a classic urn set atop a fluted pedestal. The white and gold accented architectural elements were washed with warm pink light from above. The display area

simulated a boudoir setting complete with marble floor rugs color rubbed panelled walls rich with architectural details, draperies and pictures. The line of bed linens designed by Louis Nichole was shown on an upholstered bed overwhelmed with accent pillows and lace edged coverlets.

In contrast, the Eileen West bathroom ensembles were shown in a cool, blue-white environment. The floral motif that is on the towels was used to enhance the panels on either side of the simulated doors. On an elevated platform, furnished with Victorian style wicker furniture, the softly colored pastel towels were shown in combinations. Behind a round table with beruffled chairs, — the color range of the Eileen West towels were lined up against the blue-white wall. In the center, a large displayer shows off more color coordinated linens. The collection also seemed to be at home displayed in an old fashioned bathroom setting complete with a leggy bathtub daintily raised off the white tiled floor. Period decoratives and flowers completed the vignette.

Photos: Feliciano and Durston Saylor

Dan River

Design: Dan Arje / Randy Neale

"The accessories and the total bedroom look are really driving the business today, and we feel we have been quick to respond to our customers' needs by offering the total ensemble," said Larry Queen of the Dan River Home Fashions division. The company is zeroing in on that competitive sheet and bedroom ensemble market for its strategic growth plans. In the past, 75% of their business was mass market and 25% was geared to the department and specialty stores. What they are hoping to achieve, in the near future, would be 45% mass merchants, 40% department stores and 15% for national chains and catalogs.

"We want to be known as a player in the upper end of the market," and the N.Y. showroom exemplifies the upscaling of the Dan River company. Special licensed collections like the Yves St. Laurent one are being presented in dramatic vignette settings. Each bedroom ensemble is shown on an elevated platform with a suggestive backwall, a floor treatment, accessories and decoratives. Display lighting techniques are employed to dramatize the vignettes, and plants work as dividers between the settings.

Construction: Superlative Interiors

Design: Wayne Little

The showroom is divided into a series of room-like settings which combine an in-use show with a coordinated folded and stacked arrangement of bed and bath coordinates. This Country Store concept was used to introduce a line of coordinated Early American designs which featured hobby horses and pineapple motifs in muted Williamsburg colors.

Natural pine "gondolas" and shelving units are paced around the perimeter walls, and the designer alternated the placement of the shelf units; some are set flat against the wall and others are set perpendicular to wall thus effectively serving as dividers. The natural pine floor on the low platform is repeated as a molding near the ceiling line, and the border motif that appears on the linens becomes a stenciled design under the pin molding. Decorative "antique" props are introduced into the room settings to add a sense of time and also to stimulate display ideas for the retailers. On the tee end of the gondola in the foreground, the complete ensemble is presented. It includes towels, sheets and pillow cases as well as a floor mat, and the entire color range is evident.

The merchandise on display is highlighted by the spots set into the ceiling and by the swivel fixtures that are directed down onto the display areas.

Wamsutta/Pacific

Design: Milo Kleinberg Design Associates, Inc., NY

As a leader in the luxury fiber count home furnishings business, Wamsutta/Pacific wanted a spacious and upscaled environment to house their sales and merchandise operations. The products are set out by pattern and each vignette display setting has a deep neutral backdrop and is lit with flexible, low voltage lights. The space is arranged to handle the heavy traffic that is anticipated during the market showings and still allow for easy sighting and selecting. The classic motif and the use of graphics enhance the upscale look and they work well with the no-color settings. The colors of the products are highlighted in the low-keyed display areas.

Principal-in-charge: J. Gregory Centeno
Project Director: Alan Rand
Interior Designer: Daniel DeSiena
Visual Merchandising: Albert Sardelli,
  V.P. of Creative Services
Photos: Scott Frances/Esto

Design: Milo Kleinberg Design Associates, NY

The designers were requested to create a fully flexible showroom that could be easily and inexpensively altered as marketing needs changed. Working with the company's visual merchandisers, designers evolved a system consisting of movable and reupholsterable walls, mobile platforms, and a universal, programmable track lighting grid was engineered. This system of modules was fitted into the 15,000 square foot space. To ensure the consumers' focus on the displayed product rather than on the architecture, a monochromatic black color scheme was used.

In contrast to the flexibility and rearrangeability of the showrooms area, the lightly colored marble elevator corridor with the trompe l'oeil ceiling vault creates a sense of permanence for the overall space. The stacked monitors incorporate the company's commercials into the total merchandising scheme.

Principal-in-charge: J. Gregory Centeno
Project Director: Alan Ran
Interior Design: Shari Caspert
Visual Merchandising: Stephen Stephanou/
*   Design Solutions*
Photos: Scott Frances / Esto

The Design Centre

Design: David Davies Associates, London

The Design Centre is located quite close to the heavily trafficked Picadilly Circus. This combination selling/exhibition building houses, on three levels, the "finest in industrial and craft design" from all parts of the British Isles. Home and office accessories, books, decorative papers, toys and games, dishes, flatware, ceramics, and fabrics are only some of the product categories assembled on the selling floors which resemble an exhibition area rather than a retail set-up. White ceramic tiled floors, off-white walls and light ceilings tend to make the areas open up and flow one into the next. The specially designed floor and wall fixtures combine natural wood with black lacquered metal.

In the stationery area, special wall fixtures show off the assorted gift wrap papers, —

in sheets and in packages. The adjustable rods facilitate the rearrangement of the wall units when necessary. Black metal uprights are equipped with arced shelf supports that hold up the frosted glass upper shelves. On these surfaces are displayed coordinated sets of books, binders and stationery for home or office. A low, but elevated, platform of natural wood serves as another display area under the aforementioned wall fixtures.

The floor cases are designed in wood and metal. The top shelf is glass and carries a display of products at eye level. The main wood table surface carries a selection of merchandise contained in partitioned areas. The cash / wrap counter blends with the overall fixturing concept.

Up on the second level there is a presenta-

tion of china, glass and flatware as well as kitchen appliances and cooking utensils. A small but very convenient cafe provides light repasts for those who would like to stay and shop longer. The very lowest level of the store is a full and well-supplied book shop that also includes publications, posters, greeting cards, etc. Throughout the selling space the myriad spotlights on conveniently located ceiling tracks light up the merchandise on the walls and in the cases on the floor. The light floods over to create a warm and pleasant ambience. The old building was completely renovated and redesigned by the DDA group and the HVAC systems seem to "disappear" under cleverly designed "beams" and ceiling drops. This is a tourist stop and it was designed to make it a pleasant and satisfying one.

In Soho, comfortably situated in a classic cast iron landmarked building of another century is an 8,000 square foot gallery of unique home furnishings also called Functional Art. Rich Kaufman, the owner of the gallery says, "Functional Art is a way of sneaking sculpture into a room."

Within the tall, airy spaces of the gallery the "Functional Art" is set out on elevations and risers, — placed on the beautifully restored wooden floors, — or hung on the neutral white walls. The soaring space is marked off with wood grained and stained Ionic pilasters, and the ceiling is filled with directional spots that accent and highlight the unique designs being presented.

Since this is a gallery set in a neighborhood of art galleries, the furniture and furnishings are presented in changing "exhibits." There may be a special showing devoted to a particular artist/designer like Howard Meister who designs stylized furniture welded from painted steel or Forrest Myers who created his furniture from crushed wire. An exhibit may also be a group showing of the works of several artists. The various spaces are at times used to show chairs and tables, lighting devices or decoratives. The pieces range in price and can be as expensive as $50,000. Some of the designs are licensed to select European and Japanese manufacturers for larger scale production, but only one piece in ten may be suitable for reproduction.

Photos: Joseph Coscia, Jr.

The Gallery of Functional Art

Design: Lois Lambert, Director

This unique showroom is all that its name implies. It is located on Main St. in Santa Monica, in Edgemar which was designed by Frank Gehry as a prototype for marketplaces of the future. Like Art et Industrie, on the east coast, this gallery also specializes in exclusive exhibits of one-of-a-kind furniture and furnishings designed and crafted by architects, artists and furniture makers. Just as Art et Industrie is surrounded by art galleries, this shop neighbors with the Santa Monica Museum of Art.

Though the market is limited, since the prices must of necessity be high, a market does exist for those who want something unique and original. Objects on exhibit

may range from chairs, tables, sofas and lighting to fountains, bathroom fixtures, shelving and mirrors, as well as new forms and variations in vases, pots and jewelry. The jewelry can be viewed in unusual cases designed by David Gale. For an exhibit of "Chair As Art," the presentation sought to "explore contemporary aesthetics, and functional and formal possibilities that are to be found in a chair" from the perspective of fifty artists. The works ranged from classical to esoteric to the whimsical, — and sometimes all three at the same time. Materials were as diverse as the artists and encompassed the use of steel, glass, granite, wood, acrylic, marble and found objects.

To satisfy the everchanging demands of the often changing exhibits requires a large space with movable and rearrangable components. Inspired by the Frank Gehry surroundings, the director, Lois Lambert,

uses common construction materials to enhance the pieces on display. For the chair exhibit, special risers were constructed of unfinished wafer board and the risers ran down the middle of the store's space and along the sides of the gallery. The concept was to have the exhibited chairs all facing in the same direction, — toward the viewer. The space itself has an odd angled architectural design and exposed beams float over the display area.

Lois Lambert defines Functional Art as "a blend of craft, fine art and function, — an authentic expression of art in utilitarian objects." She adds, "we don't sell any functional art that isn't unique or of a limited edition. We are not a furniture store."

A chair may be a chair, — but this is decidedly a gallery that shows and sells art for living.

Modern Living

Melrose Ave., Los Angeles, CA

Design: Michael Ladish, owner

Melrose Avenue, especially up in the 8,000 streets, is rapidly becoming a haven for furniture mavens, — for interior designers and architects, for the knowledgeable people looking for fine furniture and furnishings. Several streets away from the Design Center is Modern Living. It sits on a corner with a wide expanse of window to either side of the catercorner doorway. From outside the modest low gray brick building the viewer can see through the glass a series of unique and handsome contemporary chairs raised up on assorted size cubes. The cubes have flat black sides and are capped with white laminate tops. Each chair is positioned to present its best "side" — much like a piece of sculpture set up on a pedestal. The display suggests an art gallery rather than a furniture store and this is a furniture store set up as an art gallery.

Inside the store all is calm and serene. The carpet is taupe/gray and the walls are pristine white. A curved divider wall breaks up the retail space into a series of intimate settings, and the rear area of the store looks like and is furnished much like a multi-purpose room in a modern home. Glass blocks are used to add interest and pattern without distracting from the geometric crispness of the overall ambience. They also allow the daylight that flows through the two glassed sides to filter through the divider walls into the display areas beyond.

In contrast to the stark linear look of the architectural setting, a neo-classic framed pier mirror highlights a wall at the end of the gallery up front. Throughout the space spotlights in the ceiling provide both the ambient and accent illumination for the shop.

Photos: Martin M. Pegler

Importations Volt

Design: Yves Guilbeault Inc., Montreal

For the newly enlarged store on the fashionable, trendy Laurier St. in Montreal, the designer had a specific problem. Les Importations Volt had been a fixture on that street since 1983, but now was changing its product line — and its image with the introduction of ultra contemporary halogen lights and lamps; a new concept in home lighting that would require art and imagination to suggest the product possibilities. The design had to be different, — even revolutionary — in its concept.

The walls are gray and "textured," and carpeting — where used — is dark gray. The perimeter areas of the floor and even portions of the open floor are done in polished marble tiles, polished stones, lava stones and chips of wood and/or marble. Natural textures on the floor and simulated on the neutral walls provide an

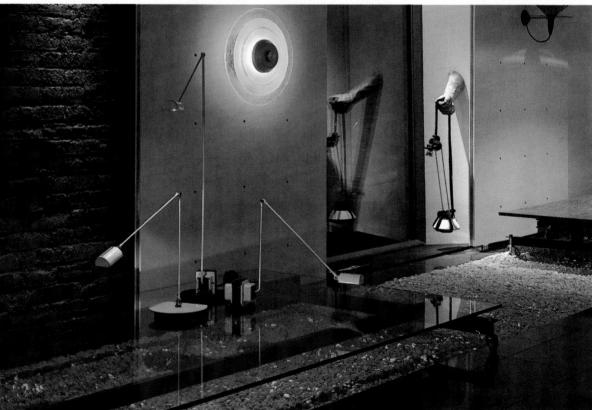

interesting and contrasting back up for the sleek, often shiny, modern lamps and fixtures. Low floor platforms are made of plate glass set in black metal armatures with wheels and the products seem to float over the textured chips below.

Throughout, the designer integrated the melange of textures, styles and historic periods in a completely no-color, gray palette to enhance the unique designs.

Textural renderings: Andre Frigon
Photos: Andre Doyon

Clodagh, Ross, Williams

Contract Magazine described this shop as "transient-violent-dilapitaded, — the look of urban streets." This avant garde setting for home furnishings and jewelry is located in N.Y.C.'s Bohemian East Village, and was designed by the imaginative and innovative designer, Clodagh, who is also a co-owner of the shop.

The store is a showcase not only for her own designs: a futuristic array of tables, furnishings and architectural lighting, but also for the work of other progressive and experimental artists and artisans. The merchandise is created out of unusual materials like oxydized copper, anodized aluminum and cast concrete. An over-scaled and dramatic cut-out provides the link between the original store and the new addition. The large exposed beam serves as a lintel over the opening. According to the designer, "the large scale

makes the space seem larger and the asymmetry lends approachability." A rusted effect was created with ferrous dust around the opening frame. The relationship of the spaces and masses within the spaces were carefully balanced to "create optimal harmony, tranquility and prosperity within the store" in the Chinese tradition of Feng Shui.

Some of the color-integrated plaster walls have been sprinkled with bronze dust to give the space a "used look" or a "beat-up look" favored by the designer. On the axis with the opening is an unusual dark green "sheet" that seems to be uncurling itself off the perimeter wall. To enhance the curl, the wall behind is illuminated. Throughout the floors are concrete and the walls are plaster and paint. The unique designs are presented against unusual textures and highlighted by spots set into the white washed ceiling.

The Light Source

Design: Fitch-RichardsonSmith, Worthington, OH

"We found that lighting stores were all doing the same thing," said Lance Vetter of Elgre Electric Supply Co. — the parent company of this new store/showroom, "and the customers were intimidated by the amount of product displayed and the lack of information available." The designers provided a more reasonable and enjoyable logic to the viewing of lighting fixtures by dividing up the large floor into "home environment" areas, and the various departments and product lines were laid out in a flow of spaces that suggests the movement through a home. There are "thresholds" that architecturally define the path and they also create visual milestones for the customers.

The ceiling plane in each department or "room" is tiered to accommodate the assortment of related products. To accentuate the light, the actual ceiling of the space has been blacked out and decorative painted panels float in space and support the lighting fixtures. It is natural to look up to see a ceiling fixture and here they are comfortably set apart from one another so each can be separately appreciated.

Each room is further enhanced with display vignettes that support the area and show life-style furnishings and decorative accessories in suggested settings. The architectural posts that serve as threshold markers are painted deep gray and the wood floor has been pickled with a peach color much like the rosy color favored on many of the partition walls. Some of the spaces are made more "livable" with accent carpets of taupe, gray or peach. The ambient lighting is low-keyed and subtle so that the product fixtures can provide the glow in the space.

Design Team: Kevin Colander, Beth Dorsey, Dan Dorsey, Susan Haller, Sandy McKissick, Kelly Mooney, Paul Nestrich
Architect: James F. Riley
Light Engineers: Larson Engineering

Sheridan

Design: Larry Bates, V.P., Visual Merchandising

Sheridan is a familiar name in Australia where it is the country's largest manufacturer of premium bedroom textiles, but it is a relatively new one in the United States. Its first free standing store was set up on the prestigious corner of Madison and E. 57th St. in N.Y.C. and this is their prototype for mall stores which are to follow in up-scale malls around the country. Sheridan carries sheets, bedspreads, duvet covers, comforters, and pillowcases plus sheets, pillowcases and bed skirts in ten coordinating colors as well as European squares, accessory pillows and fabrics.

The shopper enters through a Biedermeier-inspired opening but even before that she/he has experienced some of the theatrical displays presented in the wide glass windows set to either side of the black lacquered columns. The prints and patterns shown range from exuberant tropicals to subtle abstracts to romantic florals often designed with borders, center medallions and variations on a pattern. The store is laid out to showcase the company's "Designs for Beautiful Bedrooms" and each vignette setting, off the main aisle that runs the length of the shop, shows a complete array of furnishings for the bed in both patterns and coordinating solids along with curtains, accent pillows, upholstered pieces and even 100" wide yardage.

The Biedermeier, classic look continues with the use of straight lined, natural wood wall fixtures capped with triangular pediment accents in black. The marble floor is also highlighted with a black pattern to set off a major island display area in the center of the aisle, — just beyond the cash/wrap desk up front. Fluorescent lamps light up the raised ceiling over the center aisle and incandescent spots play up the shelved merchandise and the display vignettes, as in a showroom, along the side walls and in the rear.

Photos: Adam Pegler

Modern Stone Age

Design: Jean Jacques Ferron & Francoise Vallee

In Soho, rubbing shoulders with Art galleries and fine furniture shops is this gallery of marble and stone designs for the home. The floor is concrete set with large irregular shaped slabs of marble, and the ancient walls of this century old building are textured and finished with mottled surfaces in gray and mauve to add to the stone-like look of the space. The finish also successfully camouflages unsightly pipes and the ravages of age.

The front area of the shop is a long narrow path lined with unique designs on pedestals and cubes, and the walls are saw-toothed to channel the shopper into the main body of the store. Here, an overhanging balcony, like a space ship deck, sits over a curved service desk. The balcony serves as an office. In this central area clients are invited to sit and study

portfolios of designs available and on the wall beyond are samples of the marbles by types and colors. The rear end of the shop features a giant skylight and though still part of the gallery presentation it resembles an atelier or sculptor's studio with pieces of marble and stone mixed in with the finished pieces.

The lighting is low-keyed and dramatic throughout. The ceiling spots pick out objects on display and the surrounding dimly lit areas add to the dramatic revelation of the pieces. In addition to tables, pedestals and seats there are unusual clocks, lighting fixtures and cabinets designed by craftspersons, artists and architects like Ettore Sottsass, Michele De Lucchi and Giulio Lazzotti.

Supplementary photos: Martin M. Pegler

Hercules

Design: A. DiGiusseppe, Jr., NY

The architect/designer was called upon to convert a very uninteresting industrial space in the Sunset Park section of Brooklyn into an exciting and stimulating retail/wholesale store that would not only satisfy the local residents but prove inviting to the influx of designers and architects as well. The first step was to convert a boring concrete block facade with a few vents and one door into an eye-filling spectacle. The architect opened up the whole front, added real columns with column supports on the facade, brass channels, flags and a sign of patinaed brass with neon.

The flooring inside looks like cobblestones

to enhance the old European look and the Italian heritage of the owners, — and many of the neighbors. The sheetrock walls were painted beige and coated with a clear pearlescent finish with a squiggle pattern. A dropped black ceiling grid not only lowers the ceiling, it hides much of what is above it. The grid also supports pennants and spotlights for the displays. Black is freely applied for accents and for dramatic effect. It outlines the floors, is used for counters and bases, and black metal strips define areas and break up the window spaces.

Turquoise columns with black caps and bases serve as dramatic vertical motifs on the selling floor where the displays are set out with lots of open space around them so they can be viewed from any angle.

Galeria Shapiro

Design: Leon Escalante & Lopez Cristiani, Mexico City

Galeria Estela Shapiro is located in an up-scaled area of Mexico City surrounded by elegant hotels, high rise condos and affluent visitors. The architects decided upon a dynamic statement on the exterior of the gallery in which stark, sharp vertical planes of pale gray stucco are interrupted by one of "an aggressive purple color" that not only makes a contrast but makes a strong call for attention in its neutral surroundings.

One enters through the wide glazed doors into an area that is two storys tall with galleries off to one side and a stairway, in front, that leads to the upper levels of the

58

building. The space is filled with natural light that sneaks in through the slivers of glass sandwiched between the planes of stucco. In addition to the multiple showrooms and galleries on the various levels there is also a conference hall, two private viewing rooms and an administration area. Because the building is tall and narrow, the designers laid out the assorted viewing areas on levels that are only a few steps up — or down. The visitor never sees too much at one time but is always aware that there is more to see just beyond the square opening that leads to the next viewing area.

In keeping with Mexican tradition and with the artwork and sculpture being featured, the walls are stuccoed and white and the floors are native light wood. The well-directed lamps are never in the viewer's eyes but always on the artwork on the walls or on the clear lucite pedestals on the floor.

Photos: Antonio Pedroza

Patton-Duval

Design: John Patton

What makes the shopper stop and look first are the three brilliant awnings of green, orange and blue that stand away from the simple white facade of the low slung building. Beneath the awnings are large glazed surfaces that open on to the big, open selling floor that is divided by dwarf partitions and cabinets built around the existing square columns that form a grid on the floor.

The natural concrete floors and stark white walls, columns and ceiling are ideal foils for the flamboyant, rich colors of the mixture of functional and decorative arts located on the floor, on pedestals, in cabinets and on the walls. The spots in the ceiling more than highlight the displayed objects, they make the colors seem even more brilliant in their neutral settings.

The cabinets and walls that serve as containers and dividers on the open floor break the large warehouse space into small delightful viewing areas where pieces are arranged in harmonious groupings and there is always a vista, — an opening that beckons to another specialized cluster of art objects. The layout encourages the shopper to move from one area to the next much as one would in a museum or gallery, but here everything is "hands-on." There are one-of-a-kind cabinets, tables and chairs, many designed by John Patton the co-owner, also vases, paintings and cabinet pieces by contemporary artists like Bill Cajka, Pablo Campos, Ken De Bie, Mitsu Kato, Tammy Sioux, Gina Telcocci and others.

Photos: Martin M. Pegler

61

Chapter Two

Probably one of the most over used buzz-words today that pops up everywhere and in everything is "Lifestyle." So, we have chosen to fill a chapter with our interpretations of lifestyle shops.

According to an article in the *New York Times,* — "the term lifestyle store refers to the specialized niche that caters to the first time home buyers and the affluent owners of second homes. The stores specialize in European-inspired furniture with clean symmetrical lines, rounded edges and monochromatic and primary colors. Laminates are the materials of choice rather than knotty pine and oak. The store carries everything from dining room tables to napkin holders." We have gone beyond the confines of the *Times* definition/description, though our selections do include operations like Conrans, Habitat, Storehouse, Stor and Ikea. They are some of the largest lifestyle stores around and most of them did start in Europe. Conran's is famous in England and we are pleased to also show the newest Conran/Habitat that recently opened in Los Angeles. Physically Ikea is the largest of all the chains and the concept started in Sweden over thirty years ago. The massive warehouses, so far, are all located in the mid-Atlantic states on the east coast. Stor is out on the west coast and it is operated by International Furniture and Accessory Mart, and backed by venture capitalists. The Stor we are showing is approximately the size of four football fields!

Though the merchandise available in these stores may seem somewhat similar, since they are basically targeted at the same consumer group, what they definitely do have that is the same is the completeness of product that makes it possible for a shopper to furnish an entire home or apartment from major upholstered pieces and case goods to lighting devices down to the small necessities and decoratives one finds in a fully furnished home.

However, if life-style refers to a way of life — an image one has of whom and what one is or would like to be, and if that person dresses him or herself to portray that lifestyle, — and furnishes his or her home in the same look, wouldn't a store that provides all of the above be a lifestyle store? To add some extra sparkle to this chapter we have included some of those stores where the designer or merchant creates a look or fashion attitude that follows through from clothing to home furnishing. By this definition, as previously mentioned in the book's introduction, Ralph Lauren Polo is a lifestyle store as is Laura Ashley. We are showing examples of the new Marks and Spencer home furnishings area which joins the fashion specialty store and the food market that has become an integral part of M&S. This is not a new department store because the concept is focalized and targeted at a particular lifestyle market. Next is well known in England and not to be missed in London where almost every other shop seems to be another Next specialty store. The Next fashion image and attitude carries through from women's and men's wear to children's clothing, to fashion accessories and on to home furnishing selections. We are showing a Next Home Furnishing shop which is part of a specialty complex of Next stores located on two levels in a mall in Manchester.

Gear is an American home furnishings organization that has a particular look and style and that look extends into children's wear, children's furniture and bedding.

In any and all of these Lifestyle stores the merchandise is pattern coordinated, color controlled and often designed in modules. It is mix and match from sofa to soup strainer, from bedsheet to bathrobe, to bathmat, — and it is all in one place for one stop shopping.

Conrans
Fulham Road, London, England

Habitat

Design: Conran Design Group, London

The name Conran is synonymous with Habitat. In 1964, Sir Terence Conran founded Habitat as a lifestyle home furnishings store. It became a great success and in the next decade Habitat stores appeared beyond the U.K. to France and the United States. In 1983, he was knighted by the Queen for his outstanding contributions to design and retailing. His philosophy and attitude towards art, design and home furnishings are realized in his stores as well as through the work done by his Conran Design Group. "His

passion and acumen for good design has influenced everything from textiles and home furnishings to huge building projects and renovations. Through his designs, stores, books and catalogues he has changed the way we furnish our homes, choose our fashions and prepare our food." His New House Book, published in 1985, has become a definitive source book for anyone interested in home furnishings.

The Habitat store offers a total home furnishings package; everything from fabric and floorcoverings to kitchenware, all in a great range of color. Good design and good prices come together on the selling floors in a warm and friendly retail environment filled with display groupings by color and also completely accessorized model rooms. The out-of-town stores that Habitat has been opening throughout the U.K. are usually about 35,000 square feet in size and in addition to merchandise presentation there are attractive cafes that serve snacks and refreshments and also brightly colored wooden play areas for the children. The increased warehouse space also means larger stock levels are carried to ensure better facilities.

The in-store displays are planned by the Habitat Store Development team. "The displays are intended to inspire and provide a variety of coordination ideas, — also to encourage the impulse purchase." In-store and window displays reflect the Habitat seasonal promotions and the Conran Design Group provides the Habitat display team with in-store graphics. The store layout is deliberately arranged to encourage the shopper to linger longer in the relaxed and colorfully arrayed retail environment.

Design: Gibbons, Heidtman & Salvador, NY / Conran's Design Group

This new 50,000 square foot store recently debuted in Los Angeles and it is the largest store in this retail chain. The store is the American offspring of the famous Conran's store in England founded by Sir Terence Conran, and like its English counterparts, it offers everything for the home. Conran's Habitat is the total home furnishing store that stocks clean lined contemporary furniture as well as traditional furniture, bed and bath supplies, total kitchen and cooking equipment and even high tech lighting fixtures.

Ray Brunner, president of the 17 U.S. Conran stores has made it his immediate goal to emphasize its specialty store identity and renew its attention to the needs of his customers. The company will concen-

trate on stylish and affordable home furnishings since that is the niche that made Conran's a top retailer in the field. The new store will serve as a "launching pad for the company's new products."

The store's clean interior reflects the company's commitment to merchandise with straightforward good looks, function and affordability. Serious furniture for living rooms, dining rooms and bedrooms is arranged in room settings and the theatrical vignettes are geared to inspire solutions to home decoration. Kitchenware, gifts and toys are displayed with whimsicality and other accessories are piled high or massed out on shelves in bands of color. The "Under Glass" department features streamlined gift accessories by noted international designers.

Island displays, on the floor, introduce merchandise categories and also show them coordinated with other products. Products are stacked by color and the fixtures are angled on the white ceramic tiled floor to catch the shopper's eye and attention. The fluorescent fixtures are supported by spots that add warmth to the already brightly colored merchandise.

Ikea

From Denmark came the idea — the concept and much of the merchandise styling. Even the bright yellow and blue painted facade of the warehouse structure is right off the Danish flag. "Ikea shall offer a wide range of home furnishing items of good design and function, at prices so low that the majority of people can afford to buy them," said Anders Moberg, president of Ikea. Bjorn Bayley, president of the North American operation adds, "All our items are easy to assemble. The fact that the furniture is ready to assemble works with our self-service principle. It allows us to warehouse products easily and helps us pass along savings to the consumer. We have profiled ourselves with a certain direction in the U.S. and we want to broaden our target group — we have to broaden our range."

To entice the yuppies, the do-it-yourself-

or chests in a variety of sizes and finishes. Everywhere the signage is simple, clear, graphic, and explains how items can be ordered. The display set-ups show the flexibility and adaptability of systems or modular furniture components. The shopper is invited to mix and match table tops with bases and suggested combinations are shown in well illuminated areas on the walls above the merchandise. Also on the upper level there is a light, bright cheerful cafe that serves Danish type food at modest prices. The lower level is devoted to a warehouse presentation of accessories for all parts of the home.

Ikea thinks of everything including the children. A large, well-attended and cared for area is provided on the entrance level where parents can deposit their children so that they can play while the parents load up the conveniently located baskets and carts. Currently there are three Ikeas in the mid-Atlantic states with three more scheduled to open in 1990.

Photos: Martin M. Pegler

ers, and the second home owners, the two story warehouse structure is laid out with wide strollable aisles filled with neatly stacked bulk displays, model room set-ups that show in depth the products available at Ikea as well as style and color, or gallery walls with arrangements of chairs

Stør

Stør is another "Lifestyle" specialty home furnishings retailer with three outlets in the Los Angeles area. The warehouse buildings average 150,000 square feet of display space and the area is divided into room vignettes and a self-service warehouse space. Stør offers ready to assemble (RTA), European styled furniture and accessories including wall and floor coverings, lamps, housewares, bed and bath shops, and more. Each room vignette is fully accessorized with art, window treatments, floor coverings and accessories, — all of which can be purchased in Stør's various departments. In addition, from the display set-ups the customer can learn how to assemble products, how to measure and plan a kitchen or bathroom renovation or how to create a home business center from scratch.

Trained employees located in information desks throughout the floor can provide expert advice with no sales pressure being exerted.

After idea shopping on the showroom floor, the customer moves on to the self-select area where he/she can pick up an oversized shopping cart and load it up with housewares, cookware or decoratives for home or office. The shopper can also collect most of the furniture items, disassembled and packed in flat shipping boxes, in the self service warehouse.

There is a supervised children's play area for toddlers and younger children located near the entrance and a video room is equipped to satisfy the older kids. A baby-changing room is provided complete with bottle warmer and diaper dispenser. An in-store restaurant serves light meals, snacks, drinks and a children's menu.

Storehouse

Lenox Square, Atlanta, GA

Design: Fitch-RichardsonSmith, Worthington, OH

Storehouse sells sophisticated home furnishings and accessories for upscale consumers. This is the flagship store of the chain, and there were many problems inherent due to the physical set up and the two level space that needed remedying. The design firm was called in to redesign the space and to create a new environment that would correctly identify and express Storehouse's market position. Space planning, graphics, interior designing and merchandising were recreated using vignettes and clearly defined departments to put the customers in touch with the merchandise. One of the concepts evolved by the designers was the use of architectural partitions, on the floor, to break up the space into merchandise groupings that the customer could accept. This allows the shopper to shop the store without having "to dig through the merchandise."

Porticoes and doorways were developed as entrances into these subdivided areas. Each element is unique and conveys the idea, to the shopper, that what follows is also unique. By leaving a space between the top of the partition and the ceiling, the designers enabled the shopper to perceive the whole space and still be intrigued into exploring the spaces by moving through them.

New posters and graphics were designed not only to capture the shopper's eye and serve as a magnate to draw the shopper into the store, but to also explain the various categories of merchandise and tell where products can be found. In some areas explanatory graphics were devised to show samples of laminates or upholstery fabrics for laminated mix and match table tops and bases, case goods or customized chairs and sofas.

Photos: Craig Kuhner

The Gear

The Gear store is the "culmination of the home design philosophy" of this nationally known line of Home Furnishings that has rated special boutiques in major department stores. This free standing retail outlet is located in a rehabbed street level space in N.Y.'s Chelsea district opposite the famous Barneys store that draws affluent shoppers from all over the city and the suburbs. The high-ceilinged, 3,800 square foot space was upscaled and updated, but it lost none of the old fashioned charm that was incorporated into the layout of the store.

It is a contemporary "dry goods" store with kitchen supplies, linens and textiles,

dinnerware, giftware, bed and bath products, and even children's clothing, accessories and furniture. The natural wood flooring blends with the provincial styled wood tables and the shelves that box off the walls into selling spaces combined with display arrangements. The uppermost tier of wall space is reserved for display presentations of window treatments that combine textiles with finished products available at Gear. These vignettes alternate with large colored graphics: design suggestions to assist the shopper in coordinating and accessorizing the merchandise available on the floor and on the shelves below.

The merchandise on the tables is cluttered, clustered and coordinated for the shoppers to uncover and discover. This is a glorified and very sophisticated Country Store laid out and visually merchandised by experts; the haphazard piling up of products — the mix and match — the totality of presentation. Merchandise is specifically not ar-

ranged by price point but by the mixture of coordinated styles and colors, — by how things look together.

The Gear Gallery is part of the 100' long run of perimeter wall in which fabrics are hung over dowels that fit into notched uprights. The fabrics are arranged in pattern and color coordinated sequences.

Spotlights on the ceiling and on the fascia over the top tier of displays bring the attention-getting light to the table top settings and the mass displays of products.

At the rear of the store is Gear House; an open structure that contains Gear ready-to-wear, toys, and home furnishings for children. The look of the store is homey, warm and just right for affluent city dwellers looking for the better part of country-style living.

Photos: Sandy L. Studio, NYC

Anybody who has ever been to London or to England knows Marks and Spencer. Certain prime ministers will only buy their undergarments at M&S, and some gourmets swear by the bisquits they select in the food halls that are usually part of a Marks & Spencer operation. Though mainly noted for their knit goods and private label sweaters and ready-to-wear, the company has now completed their life-style orientation with their entrance into the home furnishings area.

To appeal to their middle-of-the-road customers and still introduce an upscaled look that most shoppers seem to want, M&S invited the David Davies Associates of London to design their new home furnishings division. Since the company now carries furniture, home furnishings, decoratives and a complete line of bedding, linens and such, the sales floor was divided up into room settings which are completely furnished and decorated with products that are available in the store.

The shopper is invited to stroll by stage
settings that show livable arrangements
under home-like lighting conditions, while
on-the-floor furniture is also grouped and
accessorized.

In the Linens area, the column motif is used to mark off an island stage in the
center of the selling space and the
perimeter walls carry the stacked packaged
sheets, pillowcases and comforters.
Natural wood floor displayers also carry
coordinated groupings of bedlinens. DDA
is strong on visual presentation and
packaging and their influence is obvious in
this new department for the successful firm.

Next

Next has been, for the past several years, a real retail phenomenon in Great Britain. It started out as small beautifully designed and fixtured shops with exquisite visual merchandising, and the shops specialized in womenswear, menswear, fashion accessories, etc. Soon, a local or a visitor to any fair sized English city could find Next shops popping up all along High Street sometimes one Next specialty store next to another or separated by two or three stores. To round out their appeal to a particular market and lifestyle the company added Next For Home.

In the Arndale Centre, in Manchester, the many different Next specialty stores are clustered together as a mini-department store and it is possible to shop men's, women's or kid's wear as well as furnish a home with fashionable accessories, custom covered furniture, pillows, lamps, paints and trim. Like most Next stores the decor

is light and natural. The floors are natural wood as are the vertical wall panels and the shelves of the floor fixtures. The walls are off-white and black metal fixtures serve as etageres to show off and hold the stock of decoratives. Spots, in the ceiling, fill the space with a warm, pleasant light. The products are arranged in color coordinated groupings so that self-selection of pieces that go together or complement each other can be readily achieved. Though it is a shop in a busy, center city mall, the compact space seems just right for selling contemporary home furnishings in a relaxed atmosphere.

Photos: Martin M. Pegler

Davies

Design: David Davies Associates, London

DDA has created many handsome retail settings for a variety of clients including Next and Marks & Spencer (in this chapter), so it seemed only the next step that Mr. Davies would open his own shop, just off Shaftsbury, in which he would showcase his own taste level, attitude and lifestyle.

The shopper enters into a long, narrow store and can either stop and shop for stylish clothes for men presented with elan and bravura up front or move further back into the light, well illuminated establishment to see many unique pieces of home furnishings assembled and casually presented at Davies. The merchandise is an eclectic mix but everything represents the fine taste level and perceptive eye of the designer.

The highly polished wooden floors give a ruddy glow that bounces off the white walls. Wall fixtures hold samples of especially selected fabrics which can be used to custom upholster the chairs shown on the floor. There is no formal set-up, — no vignette settings; the layout is planned disorder and the shopper "finds" unusual tables and chairs or decoratives. Custom designed and constructed wall units hold anything from bibelots, cabinet pieces, lamps, vases and plates to attache cases, candlesticks, accent pillows and lap robes.

The designer subtly blends the men's ready-to-wear with the Home Furnishings and it is not unusual to find shoes displayed along with home accessories and to have decoratives mixed in with suits, shirts and ties. The feeling created in Davies is that anything one purchases here is in good taste and has been personally selected, organized and presented for a client who can appreciate something different, — something special for someone who is special.

Chapter Three

A department store used to be a department store because in addition to the soft lines — the fashion merchandise, it also carried a full range of hard lines including furniture and home furnishings. Some classic old department stores have all but lost their identification as their Home Furnishing areas become only vestiges of what they once were and now, more than anything, resemble gift shops within a fashion specialty store.

Other department stores have boldly advanced and turned entire selling floors into Home Furnishing or Home Fashion Worlds, and integrated the home merchandise into their fashion presentations that appear in the window displays and the on-the-aisle displays that front the shops within the shop on the fashion floor. One of the department stores, in this chapter, has gone even further and created a free-standing store of over 80,000 square feet on one level that stands apart from the rest of the fashion store which is now housed in a new structure across the road.

The shop-within-the-shop concept is alive and thriving on the Home Furnishing floors of the major department stores. Designers like Laura Ashley and Ralph Lauren stake out their own boutiques and they are furnished and fixtured to look like mini-Ashleys and mini-Polo stores. Other noted designers or home furnishing specialists are also getting VIP treatment and thus a linen area may well combine several specialized shops around a large core area. Macy's San Francisco offers a variation on the theme. Off the main walk aisle which is enriched with island displays are assorted boutiques set behind architectural windows or platforms and partitions such as front a mall store. To one side, in a provincial romantic setting is a display of ruffles, bows and pretty accessories while opposite this shop is the sharp and stylish cool look of Esprit

with fixtures and fittings that befit the contemporary color palette of the products.

The age of specialization has reached China/ Glass/Giftware and there are complete environments to house Daum, Lalique, Baccarat, and Waterford/Wedgwood. Each rates a shop of its own and a look that is definitely its own.

For years now, twice a year, shoppers have flocked to see the miracle of room settings that grace the fifth floor in Bloomingdale's N.Y. store, just as Chicagoans rush to enjoy the Trend House built on the Home Furnishings floor at Marshall Field. The Trend House is a forecast "house" in which is presented everything for the home from a particular point of view, — with a special attitude or concept. The store's buyers shop the market for furniture, furnishings, decoratives, bedding, linens, kitchenware, — anything that goes into a home, but a concept home that management feels is the next big direction in home furnishings. In this chapter we present two recent Trend Houses.

Where possible, we have tried to find examples of floor layout; show how traffic patterns are designed to bring the shopper around the floor and how they are led by displays and/or the architectural elements that define the spaces.

This chapter also includes examples from Japan, Thailand, Paris and Utrecht as well as the width and breadth of the U.S. Some of our selections are truly "high-class" stores, some are comfortably set in the middle range, but all have treated their home furnishing floors as profitable spaces. They have invested in that attitude with the use of permanent materials like marble, fine wood and metal, and with details that suggest permanence and refinement. Look up at the ceilings and down at the floors and you'll see what we mean.

Bloomingdale's
900 North Michigan, Chicago, IL

Bloomingdale's

Design: Hambrecht Terrell International, NY

"With this store, Bloomingdale's is at the lead of two important retailing trends, — a return to permanent architecture and a renewed commitment to urban centers as important retail markets," said the late James Terrell as architect and designer of this new store. This six story operation marks the return to classic department store design with elegant spacious interiors that incorporate turn-of-the-century grandeur executed with rich materials, fine woods and marbles, promenades and soaring vaults. The architects/designers freely acknowledge their adaptations of Frank Lloyd Wright's inspirational works in the creation of the look for this store.

The fifth floor house Domestics and the architectural details of this floor recall Wright's Falling Water house with the use of large wood columns and crystallized marble. In this home furnishings area, International Style is the statement and the focus is on the unique from around the world. The products include vases and objets d'art from all over, wired and fitted in the Lamp department and rug collections centering around hand made antique and contemporary designs including one-of-a-kind dhurries, kilims and exotic imports from Kashmir. Decorative Pillows, Curtains & Draperies, Bed Linens, The Ralph Lauren Collection and Bath and Closet shops are also on this level.

Home furnishings continues on the sixth floor where the Robie House influence can be discerned in the arched ceiling with neon light inserts added that lead the shoppers down the length of the selling floor, a glorious arcade known as the

Main Course. Set off of this dramatic walkway are individual shops that include housewares, china, food, candy and the Petrussian and Espresso Bar cafes. At one end, the arcade opens up to the sparkle and shine of glassware, fine china and gifts. The floor is generally conceived in gray tones with natural woods used for floor and wall fixturing. Glass chips add a touch of sparkle and excitement to the otherwise elegant area.

The Bloomingdale sense of theatre and drama is evident in the displays that are part of the store's original layout and design. Groupings are arranged on platforms that line the major aisles, and vignette clusters appear inside the "shops" on ledges, — above the collected stock, — at the ends of gondolas, — on tables, — or encompassing the supporting columns.

Visual merchandising and display presen-

tations are part of what make Bloomingdale's home furnishings so special.

for HTI, NY
President & Creative Director:
James E. Terrell
Principal-in-charge: Robert J. Cerretti &
Harve Oeslander
Planner: Michael Kirn
V.P./Creative Principal:
Debra M. Robusto
Project Director: Will Perera
Project Architect: Mario Barone
Designers: Gunji Tachikawa, Steve Duffy,
Bryan Gailey
Project Co-ordinator: Ausma Zeidlickis
Architectural Principals: Daniel J.
Barteluce & Steve Vent

For Bloomingdale's
V.P. Director of Visual Merchandising:
Joe Feczko, S.V.M.
Photos: The Saidin Group

Woodward & Lothrop

Design: Robert Young Associates, Alexandria, VA

The newly redesigned furniture and home furnishings floor in the Downtown store is sleek, contemporary and presents furniture in room-like settings. The lighting is most important in creating the at-home vignettes, and though the partition walls are off-white and the furniture is set out on a neutral taupe colored carpet, a warm comfortable ambience is created under the effective mix of spotlights and lamp lights. The square columns with terra cotta colored caps line up on either side of the wood surfaced aisle and they serve to divide the long run of merchandise into acceptable, easy-to-see and believe groupings.

In Housewares the fabulous skylight takes

over and creates a 21st century setting for flatware. A demonstration kitchen is dramatically set at one end of the area and it is complete with work surface, cooking areas and running water. The TV monitors add another dimension to the contemporary setting and also provides viewing for all when a demonstration is in the works. Notice the TV camera up in the ceiling focused on the demonstration table.

In Columbia Mall, Columbia, MD, the 55,000 square foot upper level was completely redesigned to house all Home Furnishing merchandise. It was also to serve as a model for future branch store design; to become the signature look unique to Woodies Home Store. The Culinary Arcade (Housewares) is the centerpiece of the floor and it stretches from the mall entrance to the split escalator well that overlooks the main level. The vaulted artificial skylight hovers over the main avenue for 200 feet, and the arcade provides a vista to all the other departments through archways that pierce the flanking walls. Polished stainless steel clad columns add to the streamlined look of the space.
Photos: Elliot Fine, N.Y.

J.W. Robinson

Santa Barbara, CA

Design: Chaix & Johnson International, Los Angeles, CA

The Housewares area is divided into small specialty shops, and they are located just off the main white marble aisle. A black and white checkerboard motif sets the decorative look for the space and in the shop illustrated, the border band under the fascia near the ceiling comes into view first. The shopper then becomes aware of the checkerboard ceramic tiled floor and black squares decorate the white laminate base of the wall unit on the right. The color scheme is basically all white for walls, ceiling and floor with black accents, — the black squares. High-tech, commercial kitchen fixtures are used to hold boxed merchandise and also display the featured

items. This shop is effectively merchandised in black, red and white china and accessories.

The Glassware and Crystal area of the home furnishings floor is treated as a special shop or boutique. The walls and the hexagonal shaped tables that are clustered on the floor are finished in matte black and the insides of the wall cabinets are covered with black fabric. The floor is surfaced with a dark gray broadloom, — lush, plush — and color absorbing. The all important lighting is from fluorescent strips set in the bases of the wall cabinets and the light shines up through the trans-

luscent glass up through all the glass
shelves above. In the ceiling of the wall
units, hidden beneath the fascia, are
MR 16s to add real brilliance to the cuts
and facets of the crystal pieces and a glow
to the finer porcelain objects. Set into the
ceiling and surrounding the octagonal
recess in the lowered ceiling are spots to
highlight the floor displays.

The hexagonal platforms vary in height
but are designed to nestle or cluster and
create interesting groups of elevations out
on the selling floor. The designs and arrangements can be easily changed depending upon the products to be presented.

Galeries Lafayette

The use of high technology in lighting resolved the structural obstacle of the low ceilings encountered by the architects/designers when called upon to redesign the lower level of this Paris flagship store. The numerous supporting columns also had to be controlled to create a strong circulation pattern which would force the shopper to tour the entire floor. "The challenge to unify private vendor boutiques with the Galeries Lafayette product line required integrating a strong merchandise structure which capitalized the circulation pattern."

To update this 1910 landmark structure, the plan that evolved generated a clearly defined center aisle where major displays were set out to encourage the shoppers to venture beyond the aisled merchandise. The columns that support the cupola on the ground level of the store were used to advantage to create a double loop aisle system with a center for the prestigious private vendor boutiques. This "center attraction provides for individuality while maintaining an encompassing theme generated by the design and the colors and the materials." The generous use of granite and light colors reflect a neutral tone while not detracting from the merchandise. Colors and materials include light gray colors and black, aluminum, and lacquered details.

For Walker Group/CNI:
V.P., Senior Designer: Martin Jerry
Project Executive: Mark Bradin
Project Coordinator: Verinder Maston
Color & Materials: Kevin Rice
For Galeries Lafayette:
Daniel Mourlot, Dir. of Store Planning

Iveys

Southpark, Charlotte, NC

Design: Walker Group / CNI, NY

A two story existing department store was renovated and expanded into a three level specialty department store with the new level becoming the enlarged Home Furnishings world. To transform and incorporate the third level into a functional sales floor, the escalators with their glassed walls were extended and a skylight was introduced overhead thus creating an atrium as a central core for all three floors. The style that dominated the renovation recalls Southern Georgian traditional design but it has been contemporized and brought into the 21st century.

The fine Lalique crystal and glass is set apart in its own dimly lit boutique where the emphasis is on the sparkle and shine of the products lined up in black recessed wall cabinets backed with warm dark gray fabric. Light travels down through the glass shelves and highlights the faceted cuts of the glass and giftware. On the warm colored carpet, black lacquered pedestals and museum cases hold and show off the special pieces.

The balance of the selling floor is light and airy, taking advantage of the light that comes in through the central skylight. Major aisles are paved with white marble and the individual areas are either covered with light, neutral colored carpets or white ceramic tiles. Products are displayed on the walls, on the floor, on tables, or in window-like architectural constructions

built off the aisle. These "windows" serve as entrances to particular product areas and also display coordinated groupings of the merchandise stocked surrounding or behind the structure.

Walker Group / CNI:
Chairman/Partner in charge:
   Lawrence Israel
Project Executive: Jerry Skaee
Senior Designer: Frank Sullivan
Project Co-ordinator: Errol Pierre
Color & Material Designer:
   Karen Kennedy

Two times a year a dramatic change takes place on the Home Furnishing floor of this fine old department store. A whole house takes form on the selling floor, and from far and near shoppers come to see the Trend House and to see for themselves the home fashion forecast as it is visually presented by David Snyder, assisted by Thomas Theis and a capable staff of designers and display persons.

This year one of the presentations was McArthur's Quarters in the Hotel Manila, and the viewer, upon entering, was surrounded by a feeling of serenity and a sense of order and discipline. "The quality collection speaks temptation without flash. It exudes a sense of adventure with a traditional sense of beauty." In addition to the furniture and accessories, the "house" shows the linens, appropriate china and glassware, gifts, decoratives and even culinary supplies that blend with the concept of relaxed but refined living.

The other Trend House was called Avant Premier and that one was inspired by the growing interest in Art Deco. The collection (by ASIF) included exclusive seating by John Mascheroni, a prominent home furnishings designer. The interior combined sophistication with comfort, — severe lines with softening features, and an ambience suggesting spaciousness that invites conversation and entertaining. Zebra skins covered the Italian settees, and the Industrial Arts paintings are "ideal illustrations of the serious collector." The warm settings were embellished with exquisite moldings. The overall effect of this house was "epoustouflant" — anything and everything that would stagger and overwhelm the viewer and leave her gasping.

Fashion Coordinator: Thomais Theis
Paintings: Larry Kolb, Inc., NYC
Florals: Jason-Richards
Photos: Jon Miller, Hedrich-Blessing

Marshall Field

Design: Tucci, Segrete, Rosen, NYC

Centrally located in the Galleria mall, this new MF operation became the bridge in the mall's expansion. Throughout the store it is the "specialty store" look that creates the special quality for the store.

The Home Furnishings area is located on the third level and it is reached by escalators that criss-cross through the spacious central atrium. The floor is wood parquet and many of the walls and partitions are finished in light ash wood. Below: The Designer Shops in the Domestics area are housed in the merest of architectural frameworks to suggest houses, and the wide wood fascia, capped with a dramatic crown molding, encompasses the whole display area. The multi-mullioned window frame is part of a home-y setting and it provides a look into

a fully coordinated and accessorized bedroom vignette. The low enveloping cornice adds a sense of intimacy and warmth to the assorted "shops" and displays and also makes the space seem more human scaled.

Within the Domestics area, fully accessorized beds are set out off the wood aisle and the displayed products are contained on low gondolas behind them. The fluorescents provide the ambient lighting while the spots dramatize the presentations on the pale beige carpet. Table Linens are also shown in a wood sheathed environment and the coordinated displays on pedestals and tables are backed up with stock on matching gondolas or on the illuminated wall shelves behind.

Daimaru Ukeda

Design: Chaix & Johnson, Los Angeles, CA

Daimaru had targeted the layout, the look and the merchandising of this store toward the younger, more affluent and fashion aware Japanese customer. In rethinking the visual merchandising concepts of the store, Bill Welch, a principal in W3 Associates, who was responsible for effecting the new merchandise presentation for the Daimaru Company, had to make drastic changes from the traditional Japanese store layout. Working with the architects/designers, Chaix and Johnson, he established new department adjacencies and "the store architecture varied with the individual lifestyle environments that defined each floor."

In the Furniture area, left, a natural wood floor and a single white wall become a complete, compact, apartment with everything from bedroom to sitting area, study, dining area — and even to outdoor terrace. Beyond, on risers, an assortment of chairs.

Bedroom furnishings are presented in a gallery arrangement but the area is coordinated in a single harmonious color scheme and it suggests the interchangability of the elements. A photomural on the rear wall is flanked by drapes and overlaid with a mullioned window frame to suggest a window. Though the area's ambient lighting comes from the fluorescent luminaires in the ceiling, the recessed directional spots add to the more home-like light of the space.

The Linens department combines neatly stocked gondolas on the floor with coordinated displays elevated on white platforms. Note how the simple folded presentation in the foreground is backed up with the stock of product on the almost all glass fixture behind it. On top of the bin unit, — another lay-down display plus a cutout form wearing an appropriate garment. The look and layout of the design, — the simple presentation and arrangement of merchandise is Japanese, but the visual merchandising concepts and fixtures are universal and on target for fashion conscious consumers anywhere.

Merchandising Design: W3,
San Francisco, CA

Central Depart Store

Design: John Roberts Associates, San Francisco, CA

This store is a blend of "American/Contemporary, — Japanese/Contemporary, — and all of it inspired by Milan," says the designer. The materials used within this soaring six story structure complete with atrium, are predominantly Thai. They include local marbles and stones, composition tiles and native woods that were adapted and finished to match the samples provided by the designer.

The store is located opposite Ramkamhang University where 100,000

students are registered, and they are the major market for this store. Dominating the Bedding area is a vast raised ceiling criss-crossed by beams that contain the fluorescent ceiling washers. Around the lower, more intimate, perimeter area are displays featuring completely furnished bed ensembles including matching table drops and curtains. They are illuminated by spots in the dropped ceiling.

A palette of cool grays is used in the China/Gifts section. The marble composi-

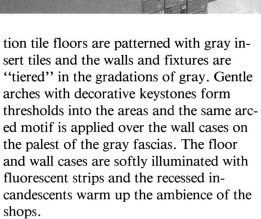

tion tile floors are patterned with gray insert tiles and the walls and fixtures are "tiered" in the gradations of gray. Gentle arches with decorative keystones form thresholds into the areas and the same arced motif is applied over the wall cases on the palest of the gray fascias. The floor and wall cases are softly illuminated with fluorescent strips and the recessed incandescents warm up the ambience of the shops.

Architecture: Casa, Bangkok
Prof. Krisida Aruvongse, Director

De Bijenkorf

Design: Fitch & Co., London

The management and merchandisers of the well-established Netherlands department store chain worked closely with the architects/planners to reposition their Utrecht store to attract the younger, more style conscious customer. Together they were able to create a selling space that reflected the well known traditional values of the company — but they were restated in a contemporary context.

The Home Furnishings area, on the lower level, is rich in presentation and auxiliary graphics. The floor is bleached beechwood and a white perforated metal suspended ceiling creates a simple but sophisticated shell. In contrast to the wood floor, a granite walkway leads the shopper to the specialty shops where the fixtures are modular white metal pipe constructions.

In the China/Table Top area, a triangular

display fixture constructed of natural wood and black metal carries a wide assortment of teapots and a black and white photomural presents the merchandise in a dramatic overscaled manner. A natural wood partition, capped with a wood framework, acts as a divider in this "shop." It holds the graphic as well as shelved stock. The overhead "ladders" support the spots that illuminate the displays in the upper areas of the perimeter wall shelving units.

Vertical merchandising and the smart wall of color blocked accent pillows are further enhanced by the splashy tumble, up front. The unique, overscaled gray lacquered ladder-back "chair" is not only a vehicle for the draped fabric but it is also a platform for some of the pillows. Behind, in a large plastic cube, the stock of uncovered pillows.

Bon Marche

Design: Robert Young Associates, Alexandria, VA

In this award-winning store, the Home Furnishings world is located on the upper level of the store under the fabulous glass ceiling that combines barrel vaulting with star vaulting — all outlined in neon. Contemporary Gothic!

The Bon is Tres Bon! White ceramic tiles pave the floors, — the walls are white and so are most of the fixtures and partitions. Everything is light — light — light, — if not in color then in feeling. Facing the main aisle are these floating glass etageres supported by the white pilasters. Hidden beneath the blue/gray caps are the fluorescent fixtures that cast their light down

through the glass shelves. The color of the deep blue/green canvas canopy that outlines a linen shop reappears on the draped tables, and as an accent border design on the aisle floor.

Inside the Housewares area, the merchandise is presented on white laminate covered tables and cubes under a stunning rotunda that recalls the ceiling extravaganza that caps the store atrium. In this view one can discern the ring of ceiling spots that highlight the assembled products, the cases that face the aisle, and the canvas canopied glassware department beyond.

B. Altman

The Home Store is a specialty store unto itself. The shopper enters through a classic portico on the marble tiled aisle, and surrounding the dramatic entrance are architectural window frames filled with mullions and Georgian fan designs. Some windows serve as display cases while others suggest a room beyond.

A gracious wide wood parquet aisle leads the shopper around the Home Store and to either side, under a lowered ceiling dotted with incandescent lamps, are livable room settings basking in home-situation light. The Market is set in the core of the floor and the space is dominated by a multi-angled rotunda filled with light. Within the confines of the wood paneled, floor-to-celing display cases that are the "walls" of the shop, is a variety of furniture and furnishings set out in a casual, relaxed, pick-me-up or sit-down-and-try atmosphere. Beautiful wood floors with handsome parquet patterns and intricate

borders, — partitions, walls and fixtures with fine furniture finishes and lowered ceilings rich in warm light all combine to become a home-like setting for the home furnishings.

Lazarus

When Lazarus vacated its old three level store in the Kenwood Mall to move into a new store across the street, a 77,000 square foot retail store with a 6,000 sq. ft. mall space was created out of the lowest level. It became the free-standing Furniture Gallery, a specialty store which showcases several top lines of residential furniture, lamps, floor coverings and a full service interior design studio.

The store designers opened the space by making extensive use of glass at the entrance and the front of the shop, and they used track lighting on 12' centers and portable walls to separate categories of moderately priced furniture. A gray mar-

ble aisle suggests the route for the shopper to follow. Along the way she/he can see room settings in flexible feature areas.

The Baker Gallery, below, was expanded to over 3000 square feet and accomplished "the interrelated merchandising and design goals" for the client. In addition there are special "series of rooms" galleries created for other lines like Henredon, Maitland and Pierre Deux.

Strawbridge & Clothier

Design: Pavlik Design Team, Ft. Lauderdale, FL

Display and visual merchandising play a major role in the merchandising plan at Strawbridge & Clothier. S&C and the Pavlik Design Team have a long and successful track record as client/designer and in these two recent additions to the venerable chain, we can see how well the architecture is designed to suit the merchandising concepts of the company. Wall fixtures and floor fixtures were created to hold stock and showcase the featured products, and the lighting design provides both a warm and relaxed ambience for the customer and sparkling accent highlighting for the merchandise.

China/Glass and Silver are set in a dimly

lit carpeted area. The cool lighting inside the pale gray lined cases is complemented by the warm spots directed onto the table top displays and the in-use, on-the-aisle settings.

In Linens/Domestics, the wall cabinets and shelving units are fabricated of a light, natural wood and the deep horizontal cuff that bands the area tends to lower the ceiling height to effect a more home-scale for the vignette displays flanked by attractively arranged product stock.

The Bath area gets a dramatic, full scale presentation and the ceiling lights are enhanced by the uplights in the setting.

Recessed in the white wall cabinets on the left is a variety of color accents that can be added to the effective black and white display.

For the Pavlik Design Team:
Principal: R.J. Pavlik
Project Designer: Luis Valladares
Project Planner: Robert Leuchter
Project Manager: Alfredo Marriaga
Lighting Designer: Constanza Kehren
Design Assistant: Fernando Castillo

For S&C:
Director of Visual merchandising:
  John Witmeyer
Photos: Jim Norris, Chicago

Burdines

Design: Walker Group / CNI, NYC

The Palm Beach store's design concept celebrates Burdine's as the Florida Store — and the easy, relaxed way of living that is the Florida lifestyle. The idea is visualized through the use of fresh colors and materials and unique signature design elements which reflect a regional vernacular.

A centrally located "gazebo" anchors a presentation of eight complete bed ensembles with the matching draperies shown on the "gazebo walls." Surrounding this focal display are low gondolas and glass binning units that carry the featured product stock.

The China/Glass department matches skirted feature tables with pastel laminate build-ups. The ceiling incandescents add sparkle and shine to the products displayed on the cool aqua table tops.

Walker Group/CNI:
V.P. Principal-in-charge: Robert Carullo
V.P. Principal-in-charge of Design:
  Martin Jerry
Design Coordinator: Meryl Foster
Project Coordinators: Raphael Banzil,
  Santos Zappala, Kris Bratton
Color & Materials Designer:
  Florence Orlando

Design: The Callison Partnership, Seattle, WA

This much talked about Nordstrom store occupies the top five floors of an exciting eight story vertical shopping center located at Fifth and Market in the rapidly redeveloping downtown area. In addition to laying out a store of 336,000 square feet, the designers had to make sure that their design would effectively draw shoppers up to the selling floors, — that their design would develop a collective store identity, — provide the latest in merchandising concepts, and also reflect and complement the store's metropolitan surroundings and the targeted market of the Centre — and the store.

For the Gift department, unique yet simple perimeter and partition treatments are used such as deep colored spandrel glass and plush cut, pile carpet. The strategically placed lighting accentuates the display of merchandise which ranges from casual pottery to fine crystal. Custom designed display fixtures are used throughout the space along with antique furniture, fine arts, area rugs and collectibles of all kinds that enhance the department's visual excitement.

The Callison Group:
Principal-in-charge, Architecture Design:
  Michael Whalen, AIA
Principal-in-charge, Interior Design:
  Charlene Nelson, IBD
Project Manager: Randall Hummer, AIA
Interior Designer:
  Christian Grevstad, IBD
Project Architect: Glen Matsui, AIA

Macy's

Design: Gregory Hribar, V.P., Macy's

The Home Furnishing floor is a mixture of small specialty shops and boutiques. The main aisle becomes the street of shops and on that aisle are decorative coordinated displays, under targeted spots, that point out the delights to be seen to either side. The Jennifer Moore linen shop is fronted by a see-through, architectural window that is as professionally displayed and illuminated as any Macy window, at street level, facing Union Square. The assorted coordinated products are presented with provincial-style furniture. Inside the shop, the natural wood floors are complemented by angled white wall units that separate the stock and also show the packaged material in colored groups. On the floor displays include skirted and covered round feature tables and a fully dressed "antique" brass bed elevated on a white platform. A dropped mirror-paneled ceiling carries the spots.

Across the aisle, the Esprit Linens boutique is, by contrast, cool, crisp and totally contemporary. The almost all white space, — from the pickled wood floors to walls and ceiling and the white lacquered modular pipe fixtures on the floor, — is washed in the light from the fluorescent luminaires. The colorful merchandise displays, up front on the partition wall, on the selling floor and along the walls are made more vibrant by the light from the myriad spots suspended off the black ceiling tracks dropped from the ceiling.

Photos: Martin M. Pegler

Chapter Four

Our selections for this chapter are as myriad and diverse as the items that go into home furnishings today. Today there are not only more "necessities" required to make a house a home, — there is also a vast range of styles, of materials — and the whole world is our marketplace to shop in. We have options and choices.

A specialty store, in this category, is often much more than a specialty store; it may be more like a "boutique" for a particular life-style, — for a particular kind of customer, — for an attitude. Some of our selections focus in on one kind or type of merchandise, and these stores are filled with a wide assortment of styles of that product that will satisfy a large audience of shoppers with needs for linens, — or lamps, — or bedroom furniture. They are truly "specialty stores," but even they aren't "pure" because they will also, probably, carry a selection of coordinates and accessories, — items that "go-with" the main product line. It is rare today that a large furniture store doesn't also feature a "lighting gallery" or an "accessory gallery" to complete their presentation.

Domain is a boutique. It carries several lines of furniture, but their whole concept is to present complete rooms with unique attitudes, and to Domain "complete" means everything from the couch and tables down to the picture frames and pill boxes that sit on the tables. At Domain, — it is total environment selling. Shaxted, a specialty store, sells linens and bath towels and the setting is contemporary while the space is limited. Kris Kelly also sells linens but is a more romantic fashion and in a larger, more open space. Night Goods, however, is a boutique designed to spoil or pamper a "bedroom" person who eats, entertains and whose leisure hours are spent in the bedroom; sleeping is only one facet of the total scene. Even Heal's, the 150-year-old English bedding company now reaches out to be a one stop shopping experience by providing more than just the beds and bedding that made them famous.

Daum, Baccarat and Villeroy and Boch are all specialty stores, free-standing on prestigious pieces of property in NYC, yet — the Lalique Collection in Bloomingdale's is housed in a "specialty shop" amongst other specialty shops on the same floor and all are part of the department store. The care that went into creating the proper setting for Lalique, — the special lighting and fixturing, — the whole design concept is intended to present Lalique in a setting that is specifically Lalique.

We have come a long way from the not so distant time when buying a stove, refrigerator or air conditioner meant a trip to a concrete and steel warehouse, owned by some "madman," where we walked miles comparing white or almond colored units lined up like the troops under cold, brittle fluorescent strip fixtures. Now, — it is color, it is graphics, it is vignette settings and sparkling lights; it is theater and the shopper is romanced. The store designer has added up-scale touches that warm up the environment and add glamour to the product. As examples, turn to Habitat, HQE and Hawthorne Appliances.

The closer we come to meeting the 21st century, the more we seem to look back to the good old days. While some retailers specialize in high-tech and modern accessories like L.S. Collection and The Shapes of Design, others are filling their shops with memorabilia and ethnic arts and crafts. Some look like New England cottages (Lillian August and Wemyss) and the ambience is warm woody and the merchandise is romantic and redolent of days gone by. The Museum of American Folk Art, Appalachian Spring and Artful Hand bring the Americana crafts to life in retail settings that suggest the past but are clearly contemporary. The growth of interest in "Southwest" both for furniture, furnishings and art gives us such remarkable shops as Umbrello and Zona. The ethnic crafts appear in Nomad, Cachibachi and Bazar Abhia and is a breathtaking example of an architectural setting that suggests the culture and tradition of the assembled products.

Many retail experts are saying that the specialty stores are where the future in retailing lies. If that is so, we believe the many examples in this chapter show that the future is bright, well lit and beautifully displayed, — and there is something for everyone.

Giles & Co.

Design: Mojo / Stumer, Roslyn Heights, NY

7500 square feet of what was once the restaurant in a pre turn-of-the-century hotel was converted into a multi-level, contemporary retail facility for the showing and selling of fine home accessories. The surrounding neighborhood is rapidly becoming gentrified and this store's appeal is to those upwardly mobile young persons who are moving into the rehabbed brownstones and are looking for tomorrow's classics today. To showcase the very best in contemporary, and sometimes avant garde, designs the one hundred year old architecture was "cleaned up," and modernized. Parts of the original construction remain to contrast with the slick, contemporary lines and materials. An arcade of brick arches that once separated two areas of an upscale food emporium that was once located here now contrasts with another arcade that is smooth and white. Old iron columns that hold up the barrel vaulted skylight over what was once The Palm Court of the hotel are now slickly sheathed in decorative red and black lacquered enclosures that add a pattern to the large rear selling space. Mezzanines, only steps up, provide special display areas as well as vantage points from which to scan the selling floor. A circulation pattern was created to bring the young shopper through all the areas of the store, and display cabinets are set up as major design elements in the total layout, and they are departmentalized. Off the major furniture floor there are specialized display sections for lighting and accessories. Throughout, the architects/designers have maintained the juxtapositioning of old and new, — in the architecture and in the merchandise presented.

Principal-in-charge: Mark D. Stumer
Project Designer: Andrew Wynnyk
Project Manager: Mike Doyle
Project Architect: Paul Sedgley
Interiors: Wendy Blumstein

Design Express

Design: Building, Los Angeles, CA

Though the interior space is sparse and loft-like as befits its former existence as a plexiglass factory, under the creative treatment of the designers, the 40,000 square foot space becomes a visually exciting and dramatically furnished retail showroom for twentieth century furniture. The layout of the design is orchestrated to move the shopper through the large space. "Space is not something you take in at a glance. It is revealed as you move through it. In a showroom you want to be left alone to make your discoveries," says Michele Saee, the designer.

As the shopper moves through the steel, wood and concrete construction, the furniture and furnishings by designers like Hoffman, Mackintosh, Mies and Stark come into view, — displayed as objects of art or museum pieces within the spaces created for them. The designer added two major partitions to the open space; one is a wood frame and dry wall partition and that one is intersected by giant, aged and rusted steel fins. The fins, in turn, divide the long window of the store front into a series of unevenly shaped bays for simple displays. The other major interruption is a group of glass and steel display cases suspended along a curved, raw plywood wall. Behind the plywood wall exposed wiring and the "commercial grafitti" is purposefully left and modular storage systems are arranged there. Off the two main aisles of the space, shoppers can view specially selected pieces to either side of the aisle.

The old factory skylights are enhanced with painted wood "cages," and the translucent material contained within the grids diffuses the daylight. Unique incandescent fixtures are attached to the factory columns and they can be adjusted to either provide ambient light or directed to highlight "staged design vignettes." The 20-foot ceiling seems lower due to the grid units over the skylights and the cruciform beams beneath them.

The Design Express ads sum it up; "Your ability to explore the uncommon Home Furnishings, — where the ordinary does not exist, — the only place where furniture and Art become one."

Building:
  Designer: Michele Saee

Assistant Designer: Max Massie
Design Team: Richard Lindquist,
    David Lindberg, Florence Lecker,
    Lohn Scott, Sam Solhang,
    Emiko Teragawa
Photos: Peter Cook
Progressive Architecture, 6/89
    Ziva Freiman

Uzzolo

Design: Darius, President

High tech lighting, furniture, occasional chairs and home accessories are on view in the lofty 6000 square foot floor space in the landmarked building that dates back to 1860. Many of the original architectural elements of the interior space have been retained such as the marble floors, the over twenty foot tall iron fluted columns that grid the floor and the wooden plank-

ed floor. They provide a great and fascinating contrast to the ultra contemporary black and steely silver furniture. The emphasis on black is so that "color and pattern won't get in the way when you're comparing one thing to another."

According to the president of Uzzolo, Darius, "We chose Soho because of its unrestricted artistic atmosphere which is so compatable with Uzzolo's unique High Tech/High Touch image. Our key objective is to create a marketplace for those who enjoy living with the best in High Tech designs, — functional furniture and furnishings, — as well as with a bit more fun."

Displays and visual merchandising get top priority, and merchandising is changed and rearranged bi-weekly to encourage frequent visits from the shoppers on the street.

Domain

Design: Cheryl & Jeffrey Katz, Boston

"Many stores sell furniture, but Domain is the first that goes beyond furniture. Our mission, our art, is to create total room environments. Exquisite one-of-a-kind settings that make your home look as though it were styled by a fine interior designer, when in fact all you did was visit Domain."

The selling floor of this rapidly growing and expanding operation is filled with completely and imaginatively arranged room vignettes where periods, styles and traditions are mixed and blended, and the settings and enriched with "precise accessories, the richest fabrics, the proper portrait, pillow or jewelry box" for an absolutely authentic ambience. The displays

in each of the stores are different, — they depend upon the materials and decorative accessories available. To create these, one-of-a-kind displays the talented design team, Cheryl and Jeffrey Katz, combine their experiences and training in architecture, store design, visual merchandising and theatre. They are fortunate that they can create their "rooms with a viewpoint" settings with the eclectic mix of product available at Domain from "antiques and quirky collectibles" to furniture and decorative accessories. "There's a sense of personality in the store," says Jeffrey Katz, "— it's not just merchandise."

Architect: Schwartz/Silver, Boston

125

In a two level space filled with light seeping through the fully fenestrated facade, the furniture store, just off Melrose Ave., is filled also with a full line of wood and upholstered furniture designed to accommodate the "easy living" of California. In keeping with the California lifestyle, the fabrics are light and mainly in natural fibers like cotton or linen.

The store is a one-of-its-kind in the Los Angeles area since it brings interior designer source furniture to the public and the pieces are set out on the open main level in clustered, coordinated groupings often without benefit of dividers, partitions or screens. Up on the mezzanine level, in the more intimate scaled space, the furniture arrangements assume more room-like relationships and the decorative accessories complete the illusion. Lamp lights and overhead spots reinforce the daylight from outside and contribute to the home atmosphere.

Visual Merchandising: Barbara &
Gerry Reingold
Photos: Martin M. Pegler

Modernage

Design: Bonnell Design / David Van Der Hurd

The new off-the-street showroom was recently opened to augment the company's 11,000 sq. ft. of loft space only a street away. Modernage is devoted to contemporary imported European furniture and furnishings and the motivating and creative force behind it all is British born David Van Der Hurd. He has been in the furniture business for over twenty-five years and his aim, since the company's inception in 1981 has been to "make good design directly available to everyone who has an interest in it — not to detract business away from the designers / decorators but to provide a source for those who prefer to do it themselves."

To prove that "design is more a way of life than business," this open space is interestingly divided into gallery-type displays on elevated platforms as well as on-the-floor groupings suggesting in-use possibilities. One special effect is the series of floating platforms on the long perimeter wall that showcases an assortment of chair designs. The long, narrow shop is subtly "broken up" by gentle color variations on the surfaces that are then divided by piers, some of which are accented with color. Above a coral "room setting" in the rear is a mezzanine that serves as an office.

Photos: Martin M. Pegler

Stylus is a custom, made-to-order, upholstery manufacturer/retailer with nineteen locations throughout southern California. The company retails everything for the living room and the family room and offers delivery within six weeks.

The average store is 5000 square feet and within that open space are shown fifty styles of sofas and chairs which can be covered in over five hundred different fabrics that are on view for selection. It is the display of the fabric samples that really is outstanding. Floor to ceiling wall units zig zag their way along the long perimeter wall and each white lacquered case contains a color coordinated range of fabrics draped over dowels that fit into the sides of the cases. On the ceiling, over each "wall," a spotlight puts the colors and patterns into sharper focus. The angl-

ed wall is visible from outside the store and from any place inside the store.

On the pale gray carpet, the upholstered pieces are arranged, not necessarily in groupings, often with occasional tables to complement them. Small decorative accessories and plants add "homey" touches. The ceiling is filled with adjustable spots that illuminate the pieces. Design consultants will work with the customer and assist in the selection of styles and fabrics.

Stylus stresses the fact that with their concept the shopper "has more choices, more options to explore — and your room will have that perfectly coordinated look you want, — all for less than you think."

Photo: Jeff Hunter

New Moon Futon Furniture

Greene St., Soho, NYC

**Design: B. Christopher Bene, Architect**

A former art gallery became a 2000 square foot display space for furniture for the space and money conscious young shopper. A 7' high wall on one side of the selling floor brings the scale of the street level loft down to one more suited to low slung furniture. This wall is modularized with niches and shelves so that furniture groupings can be related to the displays of accent pillows and other accessories. On the opposing wall, a continuous rail supports giant posters and samples of upholstery fabrics. Up front, a platform covered in sisal serves as a display stage in the window and a two level platform, in the rear, draws the customers towards the furniture arranged under a large skylight. A free standing grid also serves to separate this area from the front of the shop and suggests that something special is happening here.

Overhead rows of hanging track lights make excellent use of the high ceilings while underfoot the floor is pickled oak strip. In addition to futon furniture, New Moon also shows and sells pillows, lamps, tables, folding screens, beds and related accessories.

Contractor: Westar, Christ Laube, NY

Workbench

Design: Ed Secon

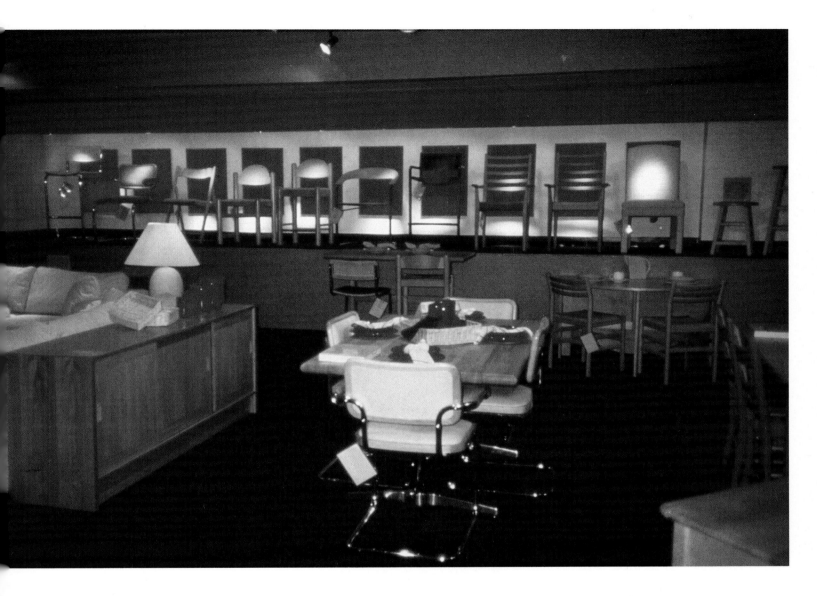

The Workbench was started in 1955 as a single shop in a second floor walk-up in Greenwich Village. Originally, the firm offered furniture in parts, but soon it was making, combining and assembling these parts in new and innovative ways. Since Warren Rubin, Chairman and founder of Workbench, preferred "a simple, clean look and sensible functional furniture," it was natural that the company would feature Scandinavian designs. In 1962, Children's Workbench came into being with the first line of furniture in the U.S. exclusively devoted to modern designs for children. Today, Workbench has 39 corporate stores and 16 franchise stores spread out across the country. "There are numerous ways to organize an attractive room without relying on a single style. Color can 'hold together' a room. Also, — consider proportions, — does the scale of the pieces relate? Rearrangements can often turn a jumble into an harmonious balance. You'll find principles like these at work in all of our stores. We consciously select and display furniture together to help you see real world design possibilities." The store's merchandise is set out in room vignettes that show adaptability and rearrangability of the products. The furniture that is presented on the floor is "designed with utility and flexibility in mind" and "simple, straightforward furniture design often helps to enhance a feeling of spaciousness." The displays may show a fully functional home office, made of modular pieces, tucked into a corner of a living room, or a bedroom combined with an intimate sitting room/den. The same piece of furniture is often available in as many as four different finishes and six variations — and they are shown on the floor. Workbench prides itself on being a "neighborhood store. It is our intention to help our neighbors continually create personal and enriching homes."

V.P. of Display and Design: Craig Barndt
Corporate Design Manager: Alana New

This End Up

Lake Forest Mall, Gaithersburg, MD

Design: Betsy Moore, Director of Design & Merchandising

"As a furniture store we are unequal in that our average store is only 750 square feet. The challenge in merchandising our stores (often in malls) is to show as many of our major living room, dining room and bedroom furniture pieces as we can in mini-vignettes. All our stores are merchandised exactly alike in order to create a constant image."

There are now almost 250 of these shops located across the country that feature the modular, crate-style, pieces of upholstered furniture and case goods made of southern yellow pine. The basic style has not changed in the fifteen years This End Up has been in business. All cushions on the upholstered pieces are removable and thus easy to clean or to replace, and the shopper is treated to a handsome wall presentation of fabric options available to them.

Most stores are open to the mall and up front a "wooden man" holds posters or signage to attract the shopper. All the accessories shown in the mini-vignettes are

for sale and there is no such thing as "do not touch." The shopper is invited to sit and sample and children are free to climb up on the bunkbeds and play with the toys and stuffed animals.

The store is illuminated with overhead spots and the lamps in the settings provide the home-like ambience.

"The true concept behind our store design is to provide a whimsical and warm atmosphere in which to help people who are making important home furnishing choices."

Dir. of Marketing, Communication & Research: Martha Pritchard
Architect: Melville Realty Co.

Glick's Home Furnishings

Design: Ray Anderson Unlimited, Dallas, TX

This store has the combined elements of classic styling with columns of light bleached pickled pine. Colonnades frame the entrances to the assorted galleries arranged around the floor such as the Americana, the Classic and the Design Center. Also, Ray Anderson's design scheme calls for beautiful backgrounds for room settings and vignettes, — the use of assorted levels on the selling floor and elevated platforms to highlight some special pieces. Special effects and adaptable lighting plans create an atmosphere that is conducive to shopping.

"A retail store must breathe excitement. It must make shopping a fun experience for the customers. It must involve the customer. It must offer ideas almost as educational presentations. Today's client wants it all and presentation must show them what goes with what." Ray Anderson tries to do all that in his store design.

Design: Ray Anderson Unlimited, Dallas, TX

Steven Pidgeon, head of the family owned company, describes his operation as "a department store of home furnishings — a super store of sorts where the customers can almost outfit an entire house in one stop." His 50,000 square foot stores, on one level often look more like warehouses on the outside, but the interiors are "slick, upbeat and sophisticated" and free standing walls delineate the spaces. Ray Anderson, who has designed four of the Pidgeon stores, combines room settings with gallery treatments, — and then adds some display pizzazz for extra attraction like neon outlined chandeliers and a carved glass staircase that leads to the mezzanine offices. Marble is used in the entry

of the store along with moire paper. "You look down this giant promenade (of miniature galleries featuring a wide range of accessories) and you think you're in the Hall of Mirrors at Versaille. Accessorized vignettes are set out to either side of the center of the store and larger room settings are presented in the gallery like spaces off to the sides. Floors are carpeted, tiled or finished with wood parquet and colors are freely used, on walls, to accentuate the products on display.

Steven Pidgeon advises, "regardless of price point, romance your product with an appealing, exciting environment that makes customers want to return again and again."

Heal's

Design: Conran Design Group, London

Heal's was established way back in 1810 as a bedding and bed shop which made beds and mattresses in a small factory on the premises. During the next 80 years, furniture and then accessories were gradually introduced, — and the result is the furnishing store it is today. The company was purchased by the Habitat/ Mothercare Group (now part of Storehouse PLC) in 1983. This Croydon store is part of Heal's expansion in the southeast thanks to its successful new trading formula and the new look that was devised for the company. The 22,000 square feet of net retail area is split between two trading floors and they are linked by a distinctive and stylish staircase and escalators that travel up to a staggering height of 22 feet. Lighting in this area relies upon the illuminated glass escalator panels and the elegant black and frosted glass uplights that were especially designed for this project by the Conran Design Group.

The interior fixtures are constructed of oak and variations are introduced to give each department a unique atmosphere. For the Kitchen area, the shelves and back panels consist of three finishes: hammerite metal, limed oak and white laminates. Furniture is presented in coordinated groupings and the accessories are color coordinated. Lighting throughout the retail space is a combination of fluorescents for overall, general illumination and low voltage, directional downlighters for interest and counterpoints.

Although Heal's did start making furniture as well as bedding back in the mid 1860s, the heart of the business has been and still is the handmade bedding. Heal's holds the warrant for supplying bedding to the Queen and her family.

Shopfittings: Mansells Limited, Croydon

Night Goods

Design: Alexia N.C. Levite, Washington, DC

Night Goods is a boutique designed to please the urban shopper, 20 to 60 years old "who is interested in pampering themselves or someone they love. It is about luxury and cozy, — affordable and outrageous, — expressing your wildest dreams and most practical needs — all at the same time."

The store consists of two showrooms. The raised, rear, area is furnished with architectural elements that suggest a comfortable bedroom; generous window frames, plus curtains and a faux fireplace. Here elements are juxtaposed against a dreamlike background of eroded walls and crumbling ceilings, — back lit in neon to reveal a twilight sky beyond. This "stage set" is suited to the wide range of bedroom accessories available at Night Goods. The main forward section of the store offers great flexibility for product display. Concealed shelving standards are set into walls, behind the drywall, creating an attractive reveal pattern. Shelves can be added, heights can be adjusted, and hangrails or waterfalls can be used instead of the shelves. The custom casework is constructed of bird's eye maple.

"Today's master bedroom is becoming the new center of the house. It is where we feel coziest, safest and as recent trends in home design indicate, it is where we exercise, eat, read, write, tune in on the media, dress, entertain — and sleep. Bedrooms of this decade are about lifestyle — and it's time for a store that satisfies our every desire for the perfect retreat" — and Night Goods does that.

Lighting Consultant: Scott Watson, Bethesda
General Contractor: State Construction Co., Kenosha
Owner: Hometown Girl, Inc., Baltimore
Photos: Martin M. Pegler

Kris Kelly

San Francisco, CA

Design: Media Five Ltd.

142

"Kris Kelly is a collage of places, times and spaces" located in 6000 square feet on three levels. A rubble rock wall extends from the entry door to the rear display area and imbues the space with a sense of antiquity. Three contemporary sand-blasted trusses transversely span the width of the first level. The elegant verdegris marble floor of the street entry yields to the provincial, pickled white oak strip flooring of the stairs and the remainder of the floors.

Wall sconces, downlights, track lighting and specialty lighting on programmable switches provide flexibility to present up to four different lighting scenes or modes.

The flooring is oak throughout and one level or space flows into the next level and space, — connecting the display vignettes. Custom designed shelves, on the walls, meet the specific packaging requirements. "Kris Kelly creates a comfortable atmosphere which provides an ease and graciousness for seeing linens displayed in a variety of evocative and romantic ways."

Project Director and Designer/Architect:
  Thomas H. Pugliusa, AIA
Project Manager: Henry G. Wong, AIA
Photos: Charles McGrath, San Francisco

Pacific Linen

Pacific Linen wanted to present an image of top value and low pricing without appearing to be simply a "warehouse" or "discount outlet" shop. The design for this 17,000 square foot store prototype was so successful that only three months later the Callison Partnership was asked to design a 5000 square foot expansion onto the new store.

The design that was evolved for Pacific Linen started as a "warehouse environment" — an open structural ceiling with utility lighting, but the space was overlaid and enhanced by "sophisticated display and merchandising systems, and bright vivid colors." The result is an inviting store, — one that appeals to the value-minded customer yet "provides a more upscale environment without being trendy or pretentious." The kiosk point of sale counters, in two prominent locations, provide focus, — good visability to prevent shrinkage, — easy accessability, and they are an important determinant in the traffic flow. They also are a pleasant visual addition to the colors and graphics of the store.

Principal-in-charge: Michael Whalen, AIA
Design Team: Bruce Brigham ASID/ISP,
Diane Monroe, Eric Stone, AIA

Shaxted

Design: Eva Maddox Associates, Chicago, IL

The challenge to the designers of this project was to house and display a variety of linen products within a rather small retail space — less than 1000 square feet. The products range in size and categories and include bed linens, decorative pillows, table linens, bath linens and accessories. To satisfy the problem of limited space and the large variety of products that needed to be shown and stocked, the designers developed a flexible modular shelving system which could be rearranged to accommodate the mix of products, shapes and sizes.

The system consists of black lacquered uprights, adjustable horizontal shelving, removable shelf dividers (for greater flexibility), and a modular base cabinet/storage component. To add some extra excitement, feature design cabinets were added to show off special merchandise.

To unify the space and keep the limited space harmonious, bronze verdegris finished grillage was used as a decorative trim throughout the store.

Owner: Stanley Ginsberg
Photo: Darwin Davidson

Marlin Lighting

Design: Portland Design Associates, London

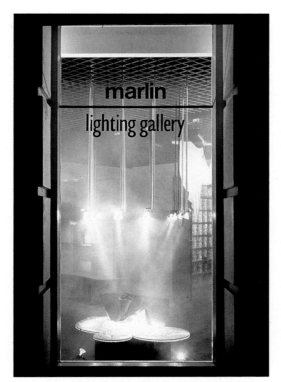

Marlin has an exciting range of home-lighting fixtures and the designers were called up to create the type of selling space that would appeal to the West End shopper who frequents Warren St. The retail store is set up on the street level and the basement is used to incorporate a lighting workshop with a demonstration area.

A cool neutral space was designed and natural materials like wood and slate were employed extensively to foster an illusion of space. The dropped ceilings not only add a sense of intimacy, and home-scale, — they also bring the array of lighting fixtures closer to the shopper. Glass block walls are added as light dividers, and touches of fantasy like the swags draped around the supporting columns soften the crisp, contemporary lines of the store's design.

Wolfman, Gold & Good

Design: Peri Wolfman & Charles Gold

In a century old cast-iron building, in Soho, where the columns on the main floor soar to great heights, Wolfman, Gold & Good brings together a unique and very special collection of table top, kitchenware and dining room accessories. The main level is long and narrow, in plan, and everything seems to be painted white except for the rich old wood plank floors and the "antique" country style tables that hold the displayed products. The columns serve as dividers and they carry the category identification. At the far end of the shop, under a skylight, is a dining room setting showing the variety of products available in the store. Spotlights on the assembled merchandise are contrasted with fluorescent ceiling washers. A white staircase leads to the basement level in which furniture and accessories are grouped in small, informal vignette settings and bits and pieces of architectural woodwork serves as dividers and frames. The lighting here, is warm and cozy as the spots are blended with the chandeliers and lamps being offered for sale.

Photos: Martin M. Pegler

Williams Sonoma

San Francisco, CA

Design: Feola / Deeniham, Archuleta, Glendale, CA

"The Williams Sonoma objective is to provide the highest level of customer service of any specialty retailer in the kitchenware market, and present an extensive assortment of unique quality merchandise in a distinctive style."

Though Chuck Williams, the store's founder, is truly a trendsetter, the store does not strain to be trendy; instead it allows good clean design to speak for itself. The store design encompasses "classic with contemporary to create a serene environment," and the warm white walls and laminated display fixtures form a neutral background for a sometimes

150

eclectic but always interesting variety of merchandise. Natural oak plank floors exude a warm, home-like feeling as do the cherrywood accented special fixtures. The carefully balanced blend of fluorescent and halogen lights bring out the full color and texture of the merchandise. The materials and finishes used in the Williams

Sonoma stores that stretch across the country and appear in the best, up scaled malls, reinforce the image of quality and timelessness as seen in the merchandise. The typical storefront design utilizes a white ceramic tile proscenium with a verde-gris marble sign band; the rest is glass.

Pottery Barn

Design: Feola / Deenihan, Archuleta, Glendale, CA

152

When Pottery Barn was originally founded in NYC in 1954, it featured inexpensive tabletop and kitchenware. In 1986, 25 stores were purchased by the Williams-Sonoma company and a new Pottery Barn was born. "The stores are now considered contemporary lifestyle stores with unique decorative accessories, selected furniture, inexpensive glassware, table top items and decorative home improvement items. All of the merchandise is well designed, honestly crafted, eclectic in origin — and well priced." Today, there are 29 stores across the country with the emphasis on the east and west coasts.

The stores are designed to showcase the merchandise, — much of it is exclusively created for Pottery Barn, — and to make shopping a happy experience. Each line of merchandise is given a special section and arranged by function, design and price, — while other products are displayed in appropriate settings to show their use in the home; be it a country home, a sophisticated apartment, a lakeside cabin or a student's room.

"We see the Pottery Barn customer as young, fashion-conscious, liking high style, change, originality, new ideas and are passionate about their homes. They are experimental and in the process of developing their own style. They like to entertain casually, but with flair and will mix take-out and home cooking with ease."

Dansk Design Store

Design: Jean Marie Knolls, V.M. Director

The company was founded 35 years ago to market designs by award winning Danish designers. Today, there is a full line of quality table top, housewares and home entertaining products "designed to all go together." All of the products are created by Dansk's 18 contract designers and the line has exclusivity as well as a consistently clean contemporary look.

The average Dansk store ranges in size from 2500 to 4000 square feet and "located only in markets with affluent, highly educated and sophisticated population." The store "will sell not just merchandise, — it will sell a concept" and it is able to be seasonal and project the image of product range to meet the seasonal needs of the customer. Like the clean contemporary lines of the products, the stores are simple, open and warm in ambience. The natural wood wall fixture system consists of 4x4 posts angled away from the white walls, and glass shelves that fit into the slots cut in the posts. Truncated pyramids of the same glass and wood construction serve as four sided floor displayers and carry feature groupings of china, glassware, pottery and giftware. One corner of the store is devoted to a Bridal Registry that features photos of the brides-to-be and their neatly listed preferences.

A central display area, under a mix of MR16, low voltage lamps and spotlights greets the shopper, up front, past the all glass facade.

Dansk feels that its customers are "uniquely attuned to design and quality" and this, the Dansk Design Store, has been created for them.

Photos: Martin M. Pegler, S.V.M.

Hold Everything

Embarcadero Center, San Francisco, CA

Design: Feola / Deeniham, Archuleta, Glendale, CA

What started in 1983 as a specialized catalogue distributed by the Williams Sonoma Company has been realized as 12 stores with more on the way. The stores contain "items that respond to the needs of people who want to organize their lives and make living easier. The store is for space conscious customers whether they're young kids in college, or moving into their first apartment or people with higher incomes who want to organize their second or third home."

The stores are arranged into specific departments or areas which deal with the customer's needs: from pantry to the bedroom, — from the living room to the garage, — from the kitchen to the developing home office. For closets there are fitted hanging and shelving systems, garment bags, shoe organizers and more, while for the office there are European style files and folders, file cabinets and desk top supplies. Like the products — everything is visually organized and presented in color and pattern coherent groupings.

The Hold Everything customer is often "a professional woman with a desire to keep her home and office in order — but with style. She is most likely a Williams-Sonoma customer."

Design: Scafer Associates, Oakbrook Terrace, IL

"Ways & Means is a store where smart people can find smart solutions to their storage and household furnishing needs — all at affordable prices."

The store is a light, bright, two-level space where all product identification can be seen from the entrance. Browsing is encouraged and "the personality of the space stirs up an emotional need to discover every item and every corner of the store." All the "fun but functional" products are selected because of their good design and their is a certain amount of "organized clutter" in the product display, — "just enough to feel appropriately crowded and give the customer a sense of excitement and adventure" along with the feeling that there is always more to come. In addition, the store provides seating, a coffee/tea bar, a resource or information center, and even washrooms with diaper changing conveniences.

Photos: Rieder & Walsh, Pittsburgh

Fuller Brush

Design: Retail Planning Associates, Columbus, OH

Located in the Towneast Mall, this award winning prototype store (I.S.P./ N.R.M.A.) offers a new "signature" look for a company that has been a household name since 1906. The "contemporary store image will effectively communicate cleanliness, efficiency and quality" and the stores will be located primarily in malls and secondly in strip centers. A major consideration, for the designers, was to display a variety of dissimilar products in a harmonious and organized environment. The space had to remain flexible enough to accommodate new and innovative merchandise.

The store uses 45 degree angled interior walls that help define several "worlds" within the 2500 square foot space. Each world is identified by a neon "call-out"

graphic. New and/or fashion products or colors are presented up front while large bulky items are placed in back. The counter/cash/wrap is set in the center of the space and it is surrounded by free standing fixtures, some on casters, — also angled for maximum visibility. The interior design uses white tiles for the floor and walls — to achieve the "cleanliness image" and light woods and vinyl wood floors for a "warm homey look." The bright primary colors and the backlit transparencies promote a fun and festive theme to the store. Overhead, indirect fluorescent lighting reinforces the store's

plan while movable spotlights and tracks are incorporated into the yellow grid to provide flexibility to the store's fixture layout.

A "house" metaphor shapes the store's entrance and the motif is repeated in the trellis over the central service counter.

Officer-in-charge: Paul Pizzini
Account Executive: James Everett
Planner/Designer: Brian Schafley
Graphic Designer: Tim Bachman
Lighting Consultant: Vince Faiella
Photos: Robert Krusey

The Gas Shop

Kilburn, England

Design: Fitch & Co., London

The British Gas North Thames selected Fitch & Co. to enhance its presence on "Main St." and also increase the customer's perception of the range and depth of product available.

A bold architectural entrance was created of ribbed stainless steel panels, a brilliant white canopy and a pair of curved glass display cabinets were placed to either side of the door. Inside the 4000 square foot shop, natural colors and materials were used to create "a warm and comfortable atmosphere" for the presentation of mainly cold white products. The multi-level shop has wood floors and the overhanging mezzanine is wrapped in wood. Black lacquered metal railings, steps and floor furniture are a sharp accent in the otherwise white environment.

Free standing system units were constructed of lacquered medium density fibre board to display and "contain" the numerous and varied gas appliances. These include freestanding displays with working fire environments.

Incandescent lighting adds to the desired "warm and comfortable" atmosphere, and enhances the floor displays.

Garber's

Design: Jon Greenburg Associates, Berkley, MI

From bathroom to bedroom, — from upstairs to downstairs, — for any room in the house, Garber's has something the shopper will need or want. In an effort to create this vast, one-stop shopping market for home decorating products, the designers turned the warehouse structure into a "department store" with wide aisles, overhead signage, dropped ceilings over specialized areas, and a lighting plan that utilizes fluorescents for general illumination and incandescents for highlighting and accenting. Low profile slatwall fixtures serve to display products on their ends while they hold stock selection on the shelves within the fixture. The saw-tooth, angled walls divide the products within a category classification into easy-to-see-and-select coordinated clusters.

The well established traffic pattern is created by the white tiled aisle. Some areas are carpeted in deep gray and other "shops" are finished with wood floors. The ceilings are painted black, and some are dropped for special emphasis. Like the floor fixtures, most of the walls are neutral gray. Display vignettes, raised up on platforms, face the aisle and show coordinated and accessorized groupings of the products stacked behind — off the aisle.

Nu-Way Plumbing Supply

Design: Jon Greenburg Associates, Berkley, MI

The stores serves a dual purpose: it is open to commercial trades as well as the public consumer. Nu-Way is a wholesale/retail showroom of residential plumbing accessories for bath and kitchen and also special areas like saunas and jacuzzis.

Here too the color palette is completely neutral: black for the ceiling, the floor pedestals and the accent stripes, — and white for the traffic aisle, the wall panels and the recessed shadow boxes. The merchandise is presented as in a gallery with the product walls or areas divided so that each design in the product line is on display and in the spotlight for the viewer's perusal. Larger objects, like bathtubs and jacuzzis are raised on platforms and presented in vignette settings with partial walls to contain them. The stock is not on the floor — but the representative samples are.

165

Habitat

Design: Jon Greenburg Associates, Berkley, MI

Habitat demanded a "help-yourself, do-it-yourself environment" for their in-stock selection of wall, floor and window coverings. With the variety of product to show, the designers still had to keep the space open and clear so that shoppers could "stand back" to consider the merchandise arranged on the tall angled wall partitions, — in the bins, — or on the flip panels.

Natural wood floors and white vinyl aisles are capped by dropped metal ceiling grids and fluorescent fixtures in white housings. The warming accent spots are attached to the grids. There are many sit-and-study centers provided for the shoppers where, perched on stools in front of turquoise laminated units, they can look at sample books or "put together" samples and chips. The overall ambience is warm, woody and relaxed.

Design: Jon Greenberg Associates, Berkley, MI

Hawthorne's specializes in custom appliances for residential and commercial installations, and the client is either an architect or builder, — or the ultimate consumer. Though the appliances are predominantly for the kitchen, the ambience has a home-like feeling due to the warm lighting and the occasional splashes of bright color in the model-room set-ups that show the products in at-home situations. To achieve an even more residential environment, the ceiling is lowered and covered with acoustical tiles. Fluorescent luminaires light up the white floors which, in turn, reflect the light up to the products set out in orderly rows. The display areas are flushed with incandescent light.

HQE challenged the architects/designers to come up with a design for a superstore that would present a dominant assortment in both consumer electronics and computer hardware. The setting and layout would need to "satisfy the consumer's total home and office electronic needs by lifestyle presentations. Vibrant colors and special architectural shapes punctuated with electronic animation, such as the IM-TECH video wall, create an electrifying shopping experience."

The merchandise is presented in separate "worlds" that are delineated by color coding, — by varied ceiling heights, and the extensive use of graphics to show and tell. The product display is designed to demonstrate features and benefits, and also — very important — involve the customers with the merchandise.

"A sense of movement and fashion is created by the store's aggressive color palette and the exciting architectural lines while the warehouse theme and fixturing philosophy combine effectively to enhance HQE's fair price image. With this store design, HQE has defined a truly one-stop shopping niche in computer and home entertainment.

Officer-in-charge: William Wood
Project Director: Gary Kaiser
Planner/Designer: Thomas Spayde
Graphic Designer: Deb Miller/Anita
   Holmes
Interior Designer: Amy Pennell
Visual Merchandising/Presentation:
   Linda Rosine
Lighting Consultant: Larsen Engineering

Impulse

Design: Walker Group / CNI, NYC

Positioned in the center core of the store and visible immediately upon entering, high margin, advanced consumer electronics attract the impulse buyers in the mall. The store's appeal is to those interested in things electronic and the design and layout of the space emphasize what makes Circuit City's Impulse so unique. The graphic elements and organized fixturing lead the shopper through the whole merchandise assortment. The interior is gray and speckled in texture, and the graphics and products stand out under the controlled lighting in the ceiling. A grid of TV screens, under the high tech framework, beckons the shopper to the rear of the store.

Project Executive: Bill Keenan
Project Designer: Jean Lugrin
Project Coordinator: Kenneth San Felippo
Senior Graphic Designer: Peter Scavuzzo

Plaza Bahia, Acapulco, Gro. Mexico

Design: Leon Escalante & Lopez Cristiani, Mexico City

A wave of the future for the electronic and computerized home of today. Undulating curves take over from the dynamic ceiling design and move the shopper through the multi-leveled space located in a mall. The actual space is long and narrow, but the dramatic gradations of neutral colors on the tiered ceilings and the bowed and banded floor fixtures tend to open up the space. The merchandise is set out within reach of the shopper, — asking to be handled and tried.

Photo: Antonio Pedroza

Waterford/Wedgwood

Manhasset, NY

Design: Neal Stewart / Design Associates, Dallas, TX

"Waterford/Wedgwood exemplifies timeless style and elegance worldwide," and they wanted a setting for their products that would express and house the faithfully reproduced, century old patterns and, "at the same time, reflect the vibrant corporate Waterford/Wedgwood of today."

The designers took traditional architectural details like columns, bases and cornice moldings and restated them in marble and wood — in clean contemporary terms. The high gloss, white lacquered columns contrast with the Canadian maple woods, and the familiar Wedgwood blue. To complement the fixed perimeter fixtures, the designers devised a series of free-standing, forward fixtures which are adjustable to seasonal or special product displays.

Low voltage, halogen lights are integrated into the display cabinets that line the wall and undershelf lighting strips shine through the clear glass shelves, — bouncing off the mirrored sides and the base shelf. A special, custom-dyed wool fabric lines the back walls and the color was selected as it best complemented the brilliant lead crystal and transluscent china.

Villeroy & Boch

Design: Dave Schoonmaker

It is a long way from that small village in the Lorraine to Madison Ave., and it has taken almost 250 years to get there. In 1936, a business and a marriage merged Villeroy and Boch as a limited partnership, and today it is a privately owned company. Though the organization is also known for its wall and floor tiles and sanitary ware, it is the Villeroy & Boch tableware and crystal glassware that are world famous. "The basic aim of Villeroy & Boch is to develop products of high value, first rate quality and practical elegance. The success is a proof that this aim has been achieved."

This shop is set out on two levels in a corner store on Madison Ave. and the products are displayed on wall fixtures that line the two perimeter walls; the other two are mainly glass with display cabinets set against the structural piers. In addition to the wall displays, there are both floor fixtures and table top arrangements that also feature Wilkens Cutlery and silverware along with the outstanding V&B designed china.

The lower level is more informal in layout and presents the more casual lines. The store is illuminated by incandescents, while fluorescent strip lights fill the wall cases with light.

Architect: Adolf Scholes, Villeroy &
* Boch Design*
Visual Merchandising: Elizabeth Knight
Photos: Martin M. Pegler, S.V.M.

Baccarat

Design: Don Baker, Baker Store Equipment, Cleveland, OH

"It is indeed remarkable that more than 200 years after our founding, the name of the little village in the Lorraine with barely 152 hearths, according to the 1789 census, should today be the name of our crystal company and that this name should be considered throughout the world as a synonym for perfection." Housed in a low lit, but brilliantly sparkling setting of dark grays and vivid red is the Baccarat Collection of fine crystal, along with Cerele china, Christofle silver, Puiforcat china and silver and Gien faience.

The main entrance floor is white marble set with black marble inserts, and deep gray lacquered museum cases are angled on the neutral colored carpet to either side of the marble. The floor-to-ceiling "walls" are also angled to show off the merchandise contained in the well illuminated cases some of which are lined with Baccarat red. Down the length of the long shop hang some noteworthy Baccarat crystal chandeliers. Spots on track light strips and recessed ceiling lamps add to the warmth and sparkle of the ambience.

Daum

Design: Philippe Renault, Artistic Director

The Daum Boutique mirrors the design of the company's first Boutique on the Rue de la Paix in Paris. The gray slate walls and floors contrast with the sparkling glass shelves and the verdigris wrought iron fixtures and furniture, — all designed by Daum. In addition to the decorative torcheres in pate de verre, the ceiling is light and a double row of recessed lamps illuminate the crystal and glassware that is displayed on the glass shelves in front of the mirrored wall. Floor cases are also finished in verdigris. The absolutely neutral setting is ideal for the changing exhibits of crystal designed by such outstanding artists as Dali and Philippe Starck.

To introduce "Les Cactus" designed by Helton McConnico, — a collection of crystal and pate de verre decanters, bowls and bookends, eight foot cacti were lined up behind the display in the all glass facade. For the opening night preview, the cacti were also set out on Madison Ave.

Design: Don Baker, Baker Store Equipment, Cleveland, OH

Though part of a selling floor in a large department store, the Lalique Boutique is designed to be the essence of the Lalique organization. Black lacquered wall cabinets are lined with gray fabric and in the center of the wood floor, on a black and gray area rug, is a fabulous table with a Lalique base. The ambient lighting is low keyed so that the accent lights, from above, make the crystal sparkle and shine. Lalique crystal is glass with the addition of at least 24 percent lead, and has a very distinctive look. Though the pieces may be clear, etched or a combination of these finishes, it is the frosted finish for which Lalique is known. It involves a combination of acid etching, sandblasting and hand polishing to achieve dazzling highlights and a satin finish.

Crystal Fox

Design: Don Baker, Baker Store Equipment, Cleveland, OH

The walls are mauve-gray and so is the carpet. A brighter, rosier mauve is used to enhance the display settings on the wall and around the supporting column which is topped with mirror. Black accents the scene; it is used for bases and pedestals and also serves as a contrast to the overall color feeling. The lighting is sharp and direct, — on the merchandise, and the accent lights are set into the valances over the case contained products, and under the fascia that goes over the glass wall shelves.

The store features crystal and glass giftware as well as small decoratives for the home.

Design: Don Baker, Baker Store Equipment, Cleveland, OH

A gallery of decorative items for the home, — the shop design makes effective use of assorted height white laminated cubes and pedestals to showcase the merchandise. The setting is neutral and the round columns add a classic quality to the contemporary design. The dropped ceiling beams are outlined with tracks of spots that are focused on the displayed items. The perimeter walls are partitioned off into glass cubicles so that, again, each piece takes on a one-of-a-kind quality, — and that reinforces the gallery concept. The wall cases carry their own highlighting spots.

L.S. Collection

Design: Bob Patino and Co., NY

The 3900 square foot shop is the flagship store for the Lazy Susan shops of Japan. In this up-scaled design by Bob Patino and Co., the merchandise is presented in a well lit space where the walls are warm white and high gloss lacquered. The floor is finished with crab-orchard stone and the wall shelving is white rift oak. Adjustable spots are set on the ceiling and they provide the on-the-target lighting for the floor displays and the wall contained products. Uplights are applied to the columns and on the pilasters between the shelves. The handsome space balances the vertical line of the columns on the floor and the piers between the perimeter wall cabinets with the long horizontal bands formed by the shelves. Gently bowed cases sit on the floor, under the shelves, and table top accessories are shown on on-the-floor tables.

The merchandise is varied; in addition to decorative glassware, barware, tea and coffee services, ice buckets and jewelry, there is also a selection of desk top accessories. Many of the products are Italian imports and are branded Stephano, Montagnoni, and Gino Cenedes.

Photos: Peter Vitale

Zona

Design: Louis & Franci Zagar

The Southwest came to Soho many years ago and its appearance at Zona was something to behold. The designers took a loft space, — narrow up front and spreading out behind, — and gave it a unique character and sense of atmosphere. Brick walls, stuccoed walls, and walls washed with color, — old plank wood floors and high, high ceilings; the architecture may be turn-of-the-century, but the effect is country casual and old west. Even the skylights that are typically old New York and the NYC skyline beyond seem to blend in with the Zona illusion.

The long counter is up front but once the shopper is past that the space opens up and seems to be divided into three major viewing areas, — one flowing into the next. The merchandise is casually arranged on furniture (for sale) and table top products, the decorative accessories and wall art all come together though there are few formal display vignettes.

The store's merchandise is rearranged weekly and each week there is a new sense of discovery for the Zona shopper; new things to find. As one shopkeeper on the same street said, "there is always something I want to buy at Zona."

Photos: Martin M. Pegler, S.V.M.

184

Umbrello

Melrose Ave., Los Angeles, CA

Design: De Wayne Youts, owner

You know that there is something special behind the old studded wood door and the heavy lattice grid that are part of the shop's facade. It just doesn't look like the neighbors on Melrose Ave. Inside, you are in the old southwest, — not the far, far west of LaLa land; plank wood floors, faience hand made tiles on the floor, rough stucco textured walls and skylights covered with canvas shutters to filter the daylight. The shopper is in a hacienda; it is a "home" cluttered with merchandise as it is, — and the products are set out in a cluster of walk through, human scaled spaces. There are actual arrangements of furniture and decoratives, there are woven rugs to set off the display vignettes and there are shelves to hold a selection of special small accessories. Spot lights add a warm glow to the interior areas while sunlight streams in through the iron-grill covered windows in the outside rooms. As in Zona, the sales space invites the shopper to browse, — to touch, — to try with no fear of upsetting a planned or rigidly set display.

The visual merchandising is as casual and relaxed as the handsome merchandise being offered. New blends with the old and some of the rare pieces are contained within wall niches that also reinforce the Southwest architecture of the interior.

Photos: Martin M. Pegler, S.V.M.

Nomad

Melrose Ave., Los Angeles, CA

Design: Helen MacGregor, owner

Nomad caters to both retail and interior design clients and it is strategically located only one street from the Pacific Design Center. "Nomad is a bright and colorful 'urban oasis' with the rarified atmosphere of a contemporary native market. The theme of the store is 'Global Style,' a design theme that transcends 'Southwest,' yet includes the Indian style in its all en- compassing range of World Tribal art."

The store offers its own collection of fur- niture and hand wovens to tiles and a gallery of native art and artifacts represen- ting many diverse tribal cultures. There is adobe finish sectional block furniture as well as hand painted iron furniture.

The fabulous collection of hand woven pillows are displayed on a stucco and wood staircase and on a wall of "steps" where each pillow, sometimes with a small decorative element, gets showcased in its own textural cubicle. The hand made faience tiled floor is "littered" with hand- loomed rugs, and at the far end of the

space, — under a skylight, a vignette bedroom arrangement. Clerestorey windows add light into the lofty white space. A bar complete with stools becomes another vignette setting in the free-to-move-around-in shop. Market umbrellas and teak patio furniture add a sunny element to the Nomad environment with the native striped canvas and well tooled rich woods. The umbrellas are featured both inside the store and in the patio just beyond the glazed doors where they provide additional atmosphere to the store's 'soukh' market which displays an assortment of native goods.

The owner/designer, Helen MacGregor is the artistic conscience of Nomad. Through her designs she "reinvented the tribe." Ms. MacGregor mixes textiles from many cultures and as she says, "I simply bring them together into one space. Nomad design brings us closer to the earth and our origins in art, color and design."

Photos: Martin M. Pegler

Bazar Bahia

Plaza Bahia, Acapulco, Gro. Mexico

Design: Leon Escalante & Lopez Christiani, Mexico City

The arts and crafts shop is Mexican in concept, — in color, — in texture and in its architectural heritage; it is also smartly contemporized. Upon entering into the warm, vividly colored interior of the shop, the visitor is attracted to the strong architectural elements; the central arch, the long stepped ramp, the massive wood surfaced steps and platforms, and the walls with their carved out niches and doorways. Centered under the massive arch and extending out towards the entrance is a "fountan/pool" and the stepped terraces serve as elevations for the flamingos and other metal sculptured birds. This is Aztec pyramid architecture — updated.

It is like being in the middle of a cubistic structure where the textures are rough but the lines are straight. The clay tiled floor is accented with natural wood grooves and the dropped ceilings form vaulted areas washed with indirect light. The on-the-floor fixtures are constructed of wood and they are also architectural in concept. The rough wood beams that stretch through the square arched openings of the wall niches and the wall dividers also bring in the old Mexican/Indian heritage of the design.

The stuccoed walls are colored in off-white, pale gold, ocher, orange, sienna and earthy brown, and the assorted colors break up the space into visual bays. The colors also highlight the alcoves for the display of glassware, pottery, ceramics, wood carvings and other decoratives for the home.

Photos: Antonio Pedroza

Appalachian Spring

Design: Arthitectnique, Washington, DC

Appalachian Spring's first store has been in Georgetown for over twenty years showing and selling American crafts and art for the home. The 4000 square foot space was recently totally renovated and new casework and finishes were added. In this shop, the architects sought more earthy feeling, — a home-spun feeling, and the basic material used is clear cedar over white washed brick.

Since the store is extremely long, a strong focus was needed in the rear to give the customers an immediate overall understanding of the space. Many crafts sold in the store reflect the highest calibre of American craftspeople and the design for the display casework was intended ''to respond to that level of craftsmanship — without overpowering it — and give the

entire store a sense of hand-made quality.'' The lighting is almost all incandescent and warm.

Above: The Appalachian Spring shop in the newly restored historic Union Station. This view is from the entrance off the East Hall. The columns, frieze work and their composition reflect the much larger scale of the architecture in the East Hall. All casework was custom designed and built. The tones of ash wood provide a soothing and warm background for the crafts objects. The architectural elements are liberally woven into the merchandise display so that the store is integrated with its site.

Photos: Pat Davis Studio

Museum of American Folk Art

Design: Marie Di Manno & Timothy Corns

This small but very cozy shop is located opposite Lincoln Center and the store showcases crafts by contemporary artists working in the folk art tradition. The space is contemporary in architecture and layout; the fixtures are simple and clean lined. The off white walls are stencilled in keeping with the Americana art look and the wall and floor fixtures are enriched with a faux marble finish in an earthy palette that complements the wood planked floors.

The mueseum cases, up front, hold some of the special craftwork, and the main counter sits in the center of the floor and contains glassed counter areas for the display of jewelry and small precious pieces. Track lights in the ceiling provide the necessary accent light for the books

and bibelots on the shelves and the merchandise in view on the counter and in the cases.

In the rear of the store, a "room" complete with fireplace and wall shelves to show off the arts and crafts in a human-scale setting.

Graining: Ruben Teles
Stenciling: Deb Mores
Photos: Martin M. Pegler

Lillian August

Westport, CT

Design: Walz Design, NY

The 2600 square foot space of this flagship for a growing chain of stores, is divided into three product areas. The front of the shop contains the Lillian August collection of "romantic" home furnishings that include wallcoverings, fabrics and hand-made accessories. The central area houses children's and women's clothing and in the rear is located country housewares and gifts. In all the areas, the free standing fixtures have steel frames with wood shelves; natural oak in home furnishings and natural pine to complement the country housewares.

The store's lighting is a mixture of incandescents, fluorescents and low voltage halogens. The fluorescent fixtures have baffles covered with duPont's Tyvek. Because the color of the merchandise is a major selling point, "color correcting lamps were used for the fluorescent and incandescent lighting to reduce the 'yellowing' of the incandescent light."

Lillian August, the designer of the products on view, draws upon Kentucky craftspeople for inspiration and her lines are mainly based on Victorian and American folk art. The shop has a cottage-like setting, designed by Walz Design as a prototype concept, and the warm woods, the fixtures, the carpet and rugs and soft pretty colors all complete the "cozy residential feel" of Lillian August.

Wemyss

displays of hand made bedding, carpets, pillows and garments are everchanging. The vaulted beamed ceiling draws the shopper to the rear as does the illuminated window.

The clean lines and soft colors of the Shaker theme provide an understated background for the products; shrimp bisque painted gypsum board walls, ceilings accented with charcoal and the pickled oak trim add charm to this small space that was designed to be flexible and enhance the character of the unique merchandise.

Wemyss is a higher end gift shop that features many hand made and one-of-a-kind gifts. This is also a one-of-a-kind shop with an almost all glass storefront with an edge lit sign. Shaker pegs articulate the entrance and show windows and the logo was developed from hand painted handkerchiefs of the Shaker era.

Entering into the 1132 square foot mall store on the pickled oak floor are set out exciting table settings and glassware displayed on Shaker "flight of shelves." The Potpourri section is carpeted and has a lowered ceiling. To define the space, the Shaker style desk houses a jewelry display and the area is fixtured with cupboards and carts. The rear space is separated by movable window walls which change the character of the rear "living" space as the

Artes

Design: Scafer Associates, Oak Brook Terrace, IL

The prize-winning store is located in an up-scaled mall outside of Chicago. Artes specializes in one-of-a-kind handmade pottery items, glass and jewelry. ''The design challenge was to create a setting where each piece of merchandise would be seen singly, — as a unique object that could compete for attention with other objects and with the space itself.''

An open inviting storefront attracts and welcomes the shopper. Soft subtle curves serve as the traffic pattern inside the shop and move the cutomers through the space, — exposing them to all the displayed products. A custom wall display system serves to showcase every item. Specially designed lighting accents the shape, color and texture of the pieces on view. The

floor is paved with dark gray slate tiles
and the floor fixtures and base units along
the wall are black lacquered, but the
shelves and platform tops are white
laminates often banded with red.

Photos: Jim Norris, Chicago

Cachibachi

Design: Ace Architects, Oakland, CA

To house an unusual collection of exotic objets d'art and home accessories, the designers attempted to create a place "overtaken by time and foliage" in the 1250 square feet of space.

There are "tall stone walls rent apart, and thick vines that clutch at space apparently once sacred, while artifacts, betraying a primitive culture, rest alongside and atop the ruins." Walls and floor to ceiling partitions are painted to simulate cloud filled skies and steel structural supports, entwined with coil vines, become mystic trees in the contemporized jungle.

The risers and platforms are cut and angled to fit into one another and create unusual stepped arrangements. Throughout, the shoppers are invited to explore Cachibachi for treasures — and pleasures.

Photos: Rob Super

Design: John Roberts Associates, San Francisco, CA

Outside, — a sweeping curved facade that reaches up two stories tells the shopper that something very special is going on behind the contemporary but classic front. Inside, — the sense of unending space, and the sense of theater is also strong. Directly in front and soaring from floor to ceiling is an architectural structure embellished with moldings that encloses the supporting column. It serves as the dramatic focal element in the store's neo-classic interior. The on-the-floor cabinets and pedestals are finished in natural woods and crown moldings finish off the taller units. The entry sweep is white marble and the carpeted area is gray, like the deep colored walls that add elegance and class to the giftware on display. The light from without seeps through the glazed openings and incandescent spots in the ceiling illuminate the products.

Maxfield's

Design: Walker Group / CNI, NYC

The design objective was "to create a prototype for a store specializing in better home merchandise, gifts and home textiles, with an emphasis on customer service and a 'casually elegant' environment that will make the customers 'feel at home'." The design had to highlight the unique mix of items, the high quality of the merchandise, — and create an image for Maxfield's which could work effectively in different regions of the U.S.

The solution included an open plan with a central articulated space to showcase special merchandise and serve as a focal point along with a clear, unique circulation pattern. The key to the design solution was a unique custom fixturing system which was developed to ensure the continuity of image. The system includes a set of bases with interchangable tops; "this system not only allows flexibility in creative displaying but can accommodate an increase of display merchandise in the future." The system is constructed of wood and designed to look more like fine furniture than a store fixture. This not only communicates a message that this is a "better store," — it also adds to the feeling of comfort, elegance and hominess that is important to the Maxfield image.

Partner-in-charge: David Wales
Project Designer: Trina Carlson
Project Coordinator: Jose Chabla
Color & Material Design: Andreas Matos
Photos: Robert Miller

Stuart Kingston

Design: Fitch-RichardsonSmith, Worthington, OH

Stuart Kingston, a family owned store, started out as a jewelry store and has, over a period of time, expanded into a series of up-scaled "galleries" that now include home furnishings, rugs, accessories and giftware. Recently the company moved into this new space which includes an historica "ice-house." There is entry into the store from the street and also from the mall at the rear of the shop.

The overall concept for the store was to create a series of mini-shops under one roof. By creating a black tile pathway that connects the two entrances, a boulevard effect was created that allows the departments to "unfold" in progression as the shopper moves through the space.

The Estate Collection of fine furniture, furnishings and antiques is located behind the Jewelry area and it was designed to

have a museum quality with an extensive use of marble and a vaulted ceiling overhead. The Rug gallery required a higher ceiling to properly present the product and the wood slatted floor represents the typical conditions to be found where area rugs are used in the home. High intensity lamps were used to facilitate truer color rendition of the rugs. The Antique Furniture Gallery was designed with built-in flexibility to allow for varying furniture vignettes. The Executive Gift Gallery is located at the other entrance and gray slat-wall is used on the perimeter walls for more adaptable display presentation, and the floor fixtures were laminated to simulate a copper patina.

Executive Accoutrements

Lane Ave. S/C, Columbus, OH

Design: Fitch-RichardsonSmith, Worthington, OH

The store, a long narrow space, was divided into a series of bays using a dropped bulkhead and a change of ceiling materials. The common area of the store utilizes a shutterwall, oak veneer cabinets and parquet flooring. As a counterpoint, signature lifestyle vignettes were established, — each depicting a different executive lifestyle since the store provides fine quality gifts, decorative accessories and functional items for use in home and office environments.

Free standing cubes direct the customer sight lines and movement through the space. Depending upon the department, the merchandise presentation varies in degree and intensity. The Traditional lifestyle, — the most recognizable executive "signature," was placed in the rear of the store to serve as a magnet. The checkout counters and office areas are all treated as part of this signature theme.

The lighting plan included high intensity, low voltage lamps with flood and spot lights, and the logo was used as a graphic restatement throughout the space.

Photos: Michael Houghton/Studiohio

The Shapes of Design

The main exterior facade is a perforated wedge that projects off the flat fascia and it carries the store name and also introduces the triangle. The key to the interior design of the 720 square foot store is the triangle. The ordinary fluorescent strip lamps that hang over each group of shelves are hidden behind black triangular wood shields. The lights serve as ceiling and wall washers and to add excitement — and change — colored gels can be set over the fluorescents to tint or tone the walls or areas of the wall. The triangle is also used in the vertical and horizontal planes, and triangular lucite pyramids serve as museum cases atop the white laminated platforms in the middle of the floor that is covered with a high-tech rubber matting. The store's palette is neutral, — gray and black. Since the designers were constricted by a tight budget, they had to improvise with elements left by the previous tenant. The floor to ceiling posts that divide the walls into compact merchandise clusters are an example of "making do with what one has."

Principal-in-charge: Shari Canepa, ASID
Project Designer: Lisa Seigman, ASID
Lighting Consultant: Delta Wholesale
 Lighting
Photo: Nick Springett

Design: Isherwood & Co., Putney, London

Studio Studio is a small, quirky shop in an old building in Kensington. Working with an eclectic mix of home accessories and giftware, — and a very limited budget, the designers created simple, inexpensive wall cases with pedimented tops, finished in black lacquer, that hold the merchandise in the tall, white space. Verdi gris metal pipe elements support the off-the-floor cases which also serve as decorative elements in the design.

To cut the ceiling height, a swag of black fabric swoops across the wall and keeps the shopper's eyes at the case level. Even the spotlights hang off a dropped light pole. A natural colored carpet completes the pleasant ambience.

Chapter Five

It's "What's up front" that counts, — and what's up front should be a good display. Display is the show and sell of Retailing; it is the attention-getter, — the shopper-stopper, — the magnet that draws the shopper into the selling space and once there turns the shopper into a customer.

Display shows what's new, what's special. What goes with what, and how the product can be worn or used and where and when it can be used. In the few seconds that the retailer has to stop the shopper strolling by in the mall or racing off to lunch on Main St. The display has to relay a battery of messages and hope that some of them strike the targeted customer. The display not only shows what is for sale, it also indicates the range of merchandise being offered and subtly states who the merchandise is for. Display creates the store's image and explains the retailer's fashion attitude, and most important of all, — it makes merchandise that might be available in other shops down and around this one seem different, unique and special.

In the more than one hundred stores that we have presented in this book, there has been a consistent emphasis on the visual merchandising, — on how the products were shown on the selling floor. In almost every instance, a display of some sort was included in the merchandise presentation. The display was often the coordinated and accessorized grouping that was elevated on a platform, up front — off the main aisle, to entice the shopper to step in and behold the wonders of the assembled products. Vignette settings, which abound in this volume, are examples of displays on the selling floor.

In this chapter we only briefly touch on the fantasy and excitement that can be the essence of a display of Home Furnishings. Realism doesn't necessarily have to be the rule; it can be more fun and more stimulating to be imaginative, to take off on a flight of fancy and show pillowcases, animated, having a pillow fight rather than ribbon tied in neat stacks and set into an armoire. The examples we have selected only hint at the creative avenues open to the presenter. Props need not be costly; materials can be recycled boards and boxes, old filing cabinets freshened with a coat of paint or musical instruments borrowed from a local marching band. What makes all of our examples successful is that they all make an image statement, — they do attract attention, and they imply that the best is yet to come, — and that is on the inside.

A really good display doesn't need to be explained. If it tells a "story," the story should be a simple one that clearly presents the whole message in the seconds alloted to the perusal of a display. If it needs footnotes and ibids, — the display is confusing the issue. A truly effective display does stop the shopper and invite a closer and more relaxed study of the assembled material, but the nuances and subleties of the message are secondary to the initial impact. As the readers turn these pages, they will notice that color and light are the major attention-getting ingredients in each of our selections and that the props, gimmicks and devices, effective as they may be, come after the well told color story is presented in good "reading" light.

Though most of our displays are window set-ups, the basic ideas and concepts can be adapted to platform and ledge treatments inside stores, — off the major aisles or, in the case of open-to-the-mall stores, in glassed off areas, up front, or as welcoming island arrangements which the shopper can enjoy from all sides as she walks into the retail space.

So, — put some fun and fantasy into your stores, — try DISPLAY.

Jordan Marsh, Boston, MA
Dir. of Visual Merchandising: Linda Bramlage, V.P.
Boston V.M. Director: Cindy Thrana
Photo: Photographic Interiors

Macy's, San Francisco, CA
Dir. V.M. and Store Design: Greg Hribar, V.P.
Creative Director: Phil Long
Window Manager/Design: Dusty Atkins

Marshall Field, State St., Chicago, IL
Dir. of Visual Merchandising: Ken Smart, V.P.
Dir. of Windows, State St., Jamie Becker
Mngr. Window Display: Amy Meadows

Bloomingdale's, NYC
Dir. of Visual Merchandising: Joe Feczko, SVM, V.P.
N.Y. Window Manager: Robin Lauritano

Bergdorf Goodman, Fifth Ave., NYC
Dir. of Store Design: Angela Patterson, V.P.
Dir. of Visual Presentation: Richard Currier

Bergdorf Goodman, Fifth Ave., NYC
Dir. of Store Design: Angela Patterson, V.P.
Dir. of Visual Presentation: Richard Currier

Gumps, San Francisco, CA
Dir. of Visual Merchandising: Robert Mahoney, SVM

Jordan Marsh, Boston, MA
Dir. of Visual Merchandising: Linda Bramlage, V.P.
Boston V.M. Director: Cinda Thrana

Woodward & Lothrop, Washington, D.C.
Dir. of Visual Merchandising: Jack Dorner, V.P.
V.M. Dir. Washington: Jan Suit

Marshall Field, State St., Chicago, IL
Dir. of Visual Merchandising: Ken Smart, V.P.
Dir. of Windows, State St.: Jamie Becker
Mngr. Window Display: Amy Meadows

Barneys, Seventh Ave., Chelsea, NYC
Creative Director: Simon Doonan

Index